Overcoming ROCD

Practical, self-help exercises to unshackle from the chains of
Relationship-focused Obsessive-Compulsive Disorder

Dr. Sunil Punjabi

D1737003

Dedicated to all the psychiatrists and therapists, who ignited the spark in me to get into this field.

Dedicated also to those therapists who do not understand the dynamics of OCD, which prompted me to attempt a book of this sort.

Dedicated also to those clients of mine who put their faith in me to help them through their struggles

Table of Contents

CONTENTS

CONTENTS

CONTENTS

Reviews

'If you know anyone suffering from ROCD, this is the book for them.OCD is a complex disorder and dealing with it with the help of a book is possible, but not easy. Dr. Punjabi has converted scientific information into an easy to understand, digestible format and has simplified the process of therapy for sufferers, so that you can work on your ROCD from the comfort of your home. Through examples, analogies and metaphors he explains nuances of ROCD that you may not find in other books. I am surely going to recommend this to my patients who struggle with ROCD and anyone else who wants to know more about the disorder.'

- Dr. Astik Mane (Psychiatrist)

'This book is a must-read for people struggling with obsessive-compulsive disorder (OCD), specifically the relationship theme known as relationship OCD or ROCD. It discusses the three types of ROCD and explains the corresponding obsessions and compulsions. It is an interactive book that offers a step-by-step approach to treating this condition. Moreover, it is comprehensive, straightforward, practical and an excellent resource for therapists who treat OCD. Dr. Punjabi writes like he's present within the book, inspiring and motivating the reader to make sense of the disorder and change things around for themselves. In addition, he expertly involves the partner throughout, helping them identify the symptoms of their loved one's ROCD and how to manage it. Finally, after taking his readers through the basics, Dr. Punjabi skilfully incorporates an eclectic approach using the evidence-based exposure-response prevention with Mindfulness, ACT and other values-based principles. A book worth investing in, highly recommended.'

- Carol Edwards, (Author, OCD Coach)

'The level of depth in this book is just amazing! The information provided on relationship OCD is by far the most in-depth I've seen anywhere. The book goes into so much detail that one would have very limited questions left. I love the idea of the worksheets, the analogies

used that make the understanding simpler and the 'letting doubts remain unsolved' part. Dr. Punjabi has successfully managed to compile the principles of therapy together into a readable source which is absolutely astonishing. This book is definitely capable of helping someone recover even without therapy, which is incredible. I wish, wish, wish I had something like this when I was struggling. Dr. Punjabi's work and knowledge is life changing and although I will always live with OCD, my recovery is ongoing thanks to him and I owe him for that. I am struggling to find any fault as a reader - he is a fantastic author and a fantastic therapist. Take it from me - invest in your mental health and use Dr. Punjabi's work as your coach, it will be the best decision you've ever made.'

-       Aimee Smith, (ROCD Client)

Acknowledgments

There are a few people whose support I would like to acknowledge for helping me put this book together. I want to thank two of my constants - my brother, Sanjay Punjabi and my friend Aditya Save, who have always been a sounding board, an encouragement and a guiding light.

I want to thank my friend, Smitha Satpute who has not only been encouraging, but has also managed my digital presence through her company WeCare Digital (www.wecaredigital.in). Her team is to be credited for the wonderful cover illustration of Overcoming ROCD, my first book, Ctrl Alt Repeat, and also hopefully, all my future books.

I want to thank Carol Edwards for always being available to discuss sticky issues with me. Her having gone through OCD herself and becoming an OCD coach subsequently, enables her to provide an extremely insightful perspective, which I am grateful for.

I want to thank Aimee Smith for her valuable inputs for this course book. While I would not wish this disorder on anyone, I do want to thank my clients who suffer from ROCD. It is discussions with them that have led to the culmination of this course book.

Lastly, of course, I want to thank my wife, Sonal, and my son, Shlok for being the steadying forces in my life, despite all that we have gone through.

Section I: Introduction to OCD and ROCD

S1C1. Introduction to the course book

Hello and welcome to this course book on Overcoming Relationship-focused Obsessive-Compulsive Disorder or what is commonly known as ROCD. This course book is designed to provide the support you need and help you deal with your ROCD. I have taken the pains to make the course book scientifically correct without any of the overwhelming scientific jargon (read gobbledygook). The language is simple and understandable even for non-native English speakers. My intention is to talk to you, talk you through your struggles, and walk with you in your recovery journey rather than preach to you from the sidelines.

This course book is also designed to make your partner more aware of ROCD. Through this course book, the two of you will learn about ROCD, how it works and what compulsions it makes you do. Even though this disorder afflicts one person, the effect of the disorder can be seen in both partners. Partners of people with ROCD are often clueless about what they can do to help with the ROCD. Lack of knowledge may lead them to enable their partners' ROCD, thereby making it stronger. Or they may push the sufferer away out of frustration. It is sad but true that breakups and divorces are common in couples where one person suffers from ROCD. Hence, education and getting a thorough understanding of how ROCD works for both partners is critical, to avoid the pitfalls.

Through this course book, you will learn how to deal with the anxiety efficiently without doing your compulsions. You will learn that the power of not needing to do the compulsions is in your hands. You will learn ways to recognize when you are triggered, what your various triggers, obsessions and compulsions are, and how to manage your anxiety through response prevention. I have provided a step-by-step process to master ERP for ROCD, along with the application of the principles of acceptance and mindfulness, so that you do not find yourself held back by this disorder. I will show you how to spot the deviousness of ROCD and how it will try to confuse you in various ways, to keep you hooked, so that you can recognize it and tackle it.

What I present to you will be simple to understand, but not very simple to implement, especially if you are trying to do it on your own. Hence, there are two critical requirements if you want the course book to work for you. One, do not just read the course book. Internalize. If you do not understand anything, re-read. If it is still unclear, reach out to me on sunil.punjabi@unshackle.in and I will attempt to clarify it for you. But make sure you understand everything well. If you read the course book cursorily, or if you misunderstand the content, it may not be of too much help.

Two, you will find twenty practice worksheets at the end of the course book. Use them well and keep monitoring yourself. You can make additional copies of the formats provided, when needed. These worksheets are the meat of the course book and the maximum benefit will come from using these worksheets extensively. Constant practice using the worksheets will help more than mere reading can. If you can get your partner involved in the process, it will be even better.

Apart from that, there is an MS-Excel workbook called 'Worksheets' that has all these twenty practice worksheets (in case you prefer the digital version), six psychometric tests (not available in the course book) and a dashboard sheet. You can download the workbook from www.unshackle.in/rocd/. (On certain devices though, the downloaded MS-Excel workbook may show up as 'Read Only' and you may have to click on the 'Enable Editing' button on your devices).

The first psychometric test is for your partner to determine if your partner accommodates your ROCD, and if so, to what extent. The remaining five psychometric tests are to measure the presence and severity of your OCD, to assess your mindfulness, to understand your acceptance levels, to check how compassionate you are towards yourself, and to test your insight. All these tests are self-administered and free-to-use tests. In some cases, the scores have been adapted to suit replication on a spreadsheet, without any change in the scoring methodology.

Please note, however, that the tests are not to be used as diagnostic tools. The diagnosis can only be made by a mental health professional. These tests should be considered as an indicator for further check up, or for confirmation of a pre-existing diagnosis.

The last sheet in the Worksheets file is a visual dashboard. The graphical representation and the consolidated scores of the first five psychometric tests will show up on this sheet. Cells corresponding to a test in the Inference column will change color when the test is completed. Red is undesirable and green is desirable. Your endeavor would be to work on yourself to turn all reds and oranges into greens.

You will need to use these worksheets to practice the techniques laid out in this course book. You will also find some additional reading resources that are instrumental to your recovery. I strongly urge you to read these thoroughly and internalize the information provided in them. In case you have any questions, feel free to reach out to me on sunil.punjabi@unshackle.in and I shall endeavor to respond to you as quickly as I can.

Your commitment to implementation will make the difference, so do commit to the completion and extensive practice of the course provided in this course book. If you have the right attitude for beating your ROCD and are willing to put in the effort, this course book will definitely help you in your recovery process.

If you have not read the Limit of liability/Disclaimer of warranty statement before choosing this course book, it is provided as Additional Resource 1 at the end of this course book. Kindly read through it now. Also, please provide me your details in the form appended at the end of this course book.

The next chapter is addressed to the partner of the person with ROCD.

To-Do:
Read AR1 - Limit of liability/Disclaimer of warranty
Provide your basic details in the form provided

S1C2. Note to the partner

Mental disorders have an effect on families, particularly relationships between couples. It is undeniable that the partner of an ROCD sufferer also suffers terribly. Having OCD is definitely not easy, but being a partner to someone with OCD is no vacation either. Especially when you are neither able to feel what the other person feels nor able to understand what to do. If you want to be supportive, you could end up enabling the partner's ROCD rather than providing the right support. If you are frustrated because of your partner's ROCD, no one can blame you, but it may worsen your partner's condition. But the fact that you are continuing to be in the relationship to help your partner through this struggle, is commendable. So, here are some things that you as a partner need to be aware of. (I have used the pronoun *he* to refer to the sufferer of ROCD and *she* to refer to the partner. These pronouns are used for the sake of convenience only. The concepts apply to all genders equally, though).

Education in OCD is a must: OCD is a poorly understood disorder and to help your partner, you need to educate yourself on how OCD works in general and how ROCD works in particular. Educate yourself on what you can do, what you can't, what you can say, what you can't and what you should believe and what you shouldn't. The more information you have, the better prepared you are to handle the disorder.

It is no one's fault: It is not your fault that your partner has ROCD. But it is not your partner's fault either. Neither you, nor your partner should consider yourselves on the opposite sides of each other. Both of you are on the same side against ROCD. Neither should your partner's compulsions be enabled, nor do you have the permission to be mean or rude to your partner because of your frustration. What is understandable is not necessarily justifiable. So, both of you need to be kind and compassionate towards the other person because both of you are suffering.

Your partner is not in control: Or let me say it differently. Your partner is not in control *right now*. Whatever is happening to your partner is because your partner's ROCD is in control. He does not want to feel the way he does. He does not want to behave the way he does. His ROCD forces him to. You may notice that your partner is not really happy. If he really liked doing what he does, wouldn't he be happy? He isn't because he doesn't want to do it, but cannot seem to be able to stop.

It is not your responsibility to fix your partner: In your concern for your partner, when your partner comes and offloads his anxious thoughts on you, you may end up using words like '*Don't worry, we will fix this*'. This is neither true nor correct. It is not true because it is offering your partner a false reassurance that you know how to fix it, which is not true. And, it is not correct because if you believe it is your responsibility to fix your partner's ROCD, it may make your partner also believe that it *is indeed* your responsibility. He may depend upon you unreasonably to get him out of it and he may blame you if you are unable to do so.

Also, if you are not able to help him through it, you may blame yourself and go down a rabbit hole of guilt that could have been avoided. You may begin to feel inadequate for not being able to help your partner. These are traps that you should watch out for and avoid.

Your partner loves you: Believe it or not, whatever happens in ROCD is not because your partner stops loving you, but because he loves you *more*. Any form of OCD affects a person because he has strong beliefs about something and OCD tries to negate those beliefs.

So, this is ROCD's way of trying to negate your partner's love for you. It is like ROCD telling your partner '*Do you really think you love your partner? Despite her asymmetrical eyes?*' And because he seems to lose the ability to distinguish between a real thought and an obsessive thought, he begins to question himself. So, I repeat. ROCD shows up because your partner loves you more, not less, as it may begin to feel.

You need to make time for yourself: This is very important. In addition to being available for your partner, make sure you make time for yourself as well. Seeing your partner suffer may make you feel guilty about having a good time yourself, but remember, you need to recharge yourself for two people. So, be kinder to yourself than you would usually be. Go for a drink with friends. Go watch a movie. Go spend time with your parents. Go spend time on your hobby. Guilt-free.

You need to have patience, have faith: ROCD being what it is, it is easy to get frustrated. But you need the most patience when your partner seems to be dead against you. Remember, if your partner could help it, he would not do what he is doing. Remember also, that convolutedly, your partner behaves the way he does because he loves you and not because he doesn't.

Saying the wrong things should be avoided: It might seem difficult to control your temper or frustration with your partner sometimes and you might end up saying something you may regret later, but they are only going to lead to making your partner's ROCD worse. So, here are a few statements that you should definitely stay away from:

- If it feels wrong to you, then maybe we should take a break.
- I am beginning to lose interest in you.
- Stop being so negative all the time
- How can you think that about me?
- How come I don't have similar thoughts about you?
- Maybe you should ask your friends if they feel the same way as you do.
- How about using Google to see if you are right or wrong?
- Love is a feeling. If you don't feel it, maybe you are not in love with me anymore.
- Other people have it worse. What are you complaining about?
- Your thoughts are irrelevant.
- Don't worry, everything will be alright.

Keep these points in mind in your journey with your partner to help him with his ROCD. Given the nature of this disorder and the impact it can have on people and relationships, it is easy to lose sight of these and end up ruining a perfect relationship that could otherwise have been salvaged with the right help. Make sure that this does not happen to your relationship by being better prepared.

In the next chapter we shall talk about the maladaptive accommodation of ROCD by the partner.

S1C3. Accommodation by the partner

When we struggle, it is natural for our loved ones to want to comfort us, reassure us and help us out. It is also natural for us to want to be comforted by them. For example, when a child is hurt, he may look to his mother for comfort and may want to be hugged. Similarly, when an adult is rebuked at work, he may seek comfort from his partner to soothe his frayed nerves. But there is a difference between healthy comforting and unhealthy accommodation. Often, that which may seem to be comforting or reassuring may turn out to be unhealthy accommodation, in retrospect.

Particularly in OCD (ROCD in the current context), comforting may take the form of enabling proxy compulsion, offering reassurance, enabling avoidance and so on. While some form of support from your partner is understandable, if the expected support makes you feel less anxious, and if providing such support requires your partner to make more than normal adjustments, then the accommodation might be unhealthy.

For example, does your partner make small decisions for you that you should be making yourself? Or does your partner take up more responsibilities on herself because some of them cause you anxiety? If yes, these could be indications of unhealthy accommodation. It might seem like a perfectly normal expectation to you and your mind might say that if the situation was reversed, you would do the same. However, the drain it causes on your partner may not be visible to you. Not to mention the harm it is doing to you by strengthening your ROCD further.

Pinto et al (2012) developed a scale called the Family Accommodation Scale for Obsessive-Compulsive Disorder (FAS) for assessing the accommodation provided by the family members of people with OCD. The self-rated version (FAS-SR) has been provided with the permission of the authors as PT6 in the Worksheets file that needs to be taken by your partner. Higher scores indicate more accommodation, which needs to be reduced.

The next chapter will provide the basic information you need to know about OCD.

To-Do:
Get your partner to take PT1 - the FAS-SR test

S1C4. Introduction to OCD

OCD or obsessive-compulsive disorder is a severely debilitating mental disorder that affects 2.5-3% of the population (Robbins, et al., 2019). Understanding the three words that make up obsessive-compulsive disorder can give us a better understanding of the disorder. The first word is *obsessive*, which comes from obsessions. Obsessions could be in the form of thoughts, images, impulses or urges (American Psychiatric Association, 2013), or even dreams, but for simplicity's sake, we shall club them together and refer to them as thoughts. Obsessions are thoughts that are intrusive, disturbing and sticky.

Intrusive, because they pop out of nowhere, when you least expect them. Disturbing, because the content is never pleasant. It is always about something bad that may happen, often extreme. Sticky, because the more you try to get rid of them, the more they seem to refuse to leave. For example, getting an impulse to hurt someone is an obsession. Or, getting a thought that you may not have locked your house door is an obsession. Or, in the case of ROCD, getting a thought that your partner may be cheating on you is an obsession.

These thoughts may cause unpleasant feelings such as extreme anxiety, guilt, sadness, boredom, restlessness, disgust, self-loathing, or self-criticism, which are again intrusive. Remember that these are just your emotions and these emotions are intrusive too. They accompany your intrusive thoughts and no matter what you do to make them go away, they don't.

For example, you get a thought that you are not in love with your partner. That is an intrusive thought. When you talk to her, you either feel annoyed or bored. Your mind tells you, if really loved her you would not feel bored or annoyed. These emotions don't go away when you try to make them go away.

Through trial and error, you may have identified some actions that initially help relieve the intrusive emotions caused by these thoughts and even make the thoughts come unstuck. These actions, which may be physical or mental, are compulsions. The second word *compulsive* comes from compulsions. Compulsions are physical or mental actions you may end up doing to neutralize your obsessions (American Psychiatric

Association, 2013). For example, avoiding sharp objects to prevent hurting someone is a compulsion. Going back to check if you have locked the house door and checking it multiple times, is a compulsion. In ROCD, constant monitoring of your partner's whereabouts, social media and mobile phone activity (to catch her in the act of cheating), is a compulsion.

Interestingly, everyone (even someone without OCD) has intrusive thoughts. Julien, et al. (2009) conducted a study with two groups - students and OCD patients, and found that both groups had intrusive thoughts. Abramowitz et al., (2014) quoted studies in their paper stating that up to 90% of people experience intrusive thoughts similar to obsessions in OCD.

Like, when you leave a restaurant, you may suddenly get an intrusive thought of having left your wallet or mobile phone back in the restaurant. It may cause you to quickly check if you do have the wallet or mobile phone on you. When you find that you do have it, you may forget about it. But for a person with OCD the thought may get obsessive and he may have to do the same compulsion repeatedly to deal with the obsession. The compulsion may provide temporary relief and then the obsession may return. This may lead to a repetitive cycle of obsession-anxiety-compulsion-and relief as shown in figure 1.4.1.

Figure 1.4.1: The anxiety cycle

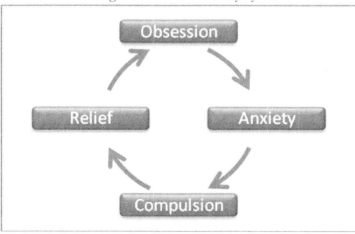

Eventually this cycle may repeat many times over and may begin to cause dysfunctionality. This dysfunctionality may extend to work, family, relationships, studies, or anything else that is important to him.

That is when it becomes a disorder, which is the third word - *disorder*.

To recap, obsessions are intrusive, disturbing and sticky thoughts that may cause intrusive emotions. Compulsions are physical or mental actions that are performed to deal with the intrusive emotions. And disorder is when this cycle needs to be completed repeatedly, leading to dysfunctionality in various aspects of life.

OCD belongs to a class of mental disorders called neurotic disorders. Neurotic disorders are those where the sufferer understands the irrationality of his thoughts but is not able to modify his behavior. Disorders like anxiety, depression, OCD, PTSD are all neurotic disorders. The sufferer knows that his actions are unhealthy and unhelpful but is not able to stop himself from doing them.

Thus, an OCD sufferer may know that his thoughts about wanting to harm someone are irrational because he does not really want to harm anyone. But the thoughts are so strong that he may not able to dismiss them. Further, he also knows that he should not be avoiding knives and other pointed objects but he cannot bring himself to handle these objects without becoming anxious.

People are often confused about what an obsession is and what a compulsion is. The confusion is caused by the presence of many mental compulsions. This may often lead to treating one like the other. In a disorder that is anyway confusing even if everything is laid out on a platter, such confusion about the building blocks itself can make the recovery process more difficult. I have therefore created an exercise to help you understand the difference.

At the end of this course book you will find Worksheet 1 for both of you to test yourselves on whether or not you can distinguish between obsessions and compulsions. The same worksheet is also available in the MS Excel workbook called Worksheets. Before moving to the next chapter, complete Worksheet 1 to get a better understanding of the difference. Move to the next chapter only if you have an accurate understanding of the difference between obsessions and compulsions.

In the next chapter we will look at a few types of OCD.

To-Do:
Try WS1 - the obsessions or compulsions exercise

S1C5. Types of presentations in OCD

Strictly from a clinical perspective, OCD is not broken down into its various subtypes. When psychiatrists diagnose a person with OCD, OCD is OCD. Neither more, nor less. Since treatment is not different for different types of OCD, the distinctions are moot. Even the Diagnostic and Statistical Manual of Mental Disorders, Fifth Edition (DSM-5) does not recognize or list the different subtypes of OCD as separate disorders.

However, some common obsessions and compulsions have facilitated the creation of several sub-divisions, referred to as presentations. OCD affects different people differently. Even within a specific presentation of OCD, there may be elements of various other presentations present. Since it is possible that you may be suffering from some elements of other presentations of OCD as well, do pay attention to the various presentations discussed and see if you can identify traces of any along with your ROCD.

Contamination OCD: In Contamination OCD, the person may get intrusive thoughts about contamination through germs or becoming sick, or some fear about cleanliness through contact (Rachman, 2004). It could be an aversion to dirt, dust, chemicals, or bodily fluids - anything. It is estimated that 26.5% of OCD cases are of the contamination theme (Foa et al, 2005). In another study, Abramowitz et al., (2008) found that contamination fears are seen in 55% to 58% of the cases.

Mental Contamination: In Mental Contamination OCD, the person may get a thought that he may consider sinful or pervert or dirty, which may lead to shame, or guilt. He may then engage in washing rituals to make the thought go away (Coughtrey et al., 2012). The obsession may not be about physical cleanliness, but the compulsions may be physical. The thoughts could be about harm or they could be sexual in nature. But the compulsion may be to physically wash and clean until the thoughts go away.

Checking OCD: This is another common form of OCD (Rachman & Hodgson, 1980), with 28.8% of patients reporting checking as a compulsion (Foa et al, 2005). People with Checking OCD may obsess over making sure that they do nothing that may harm either them or others. They may check if the appliances are turned off, if the gas stove is turned off, if the lights are switched off, if the car is locked, if the door is locked, etc.

Symmetry/Ordering OCD: In this presentation, the person may obsess over symmetry and order (Radomsky, & Rachman, 2004); asymmetry or disorderliness may cause discomfort and anxiety (Abramowitz et al., 2008). Thus, if the person has an itch on one side of the face, he might scratch that and then, just to maintain symmetry, he may need to scratch the other side as well. Or, if there is a picture on the wall that is not properly centered, it may cause distress, until it is straightened.

Just Right OCD: In this, the person may need to repeat an activity until he feels 'just right' about it, or else he may feel uncomfortable (Coles & Ravid, 2016). He may need to open and shut doors, walk in and out of the room, read the same sentence in a book, or repeat some other activity multiple times. Unless he gets the 'just right' feeling, he may not be satisfied and may continue to do the compulsions.

These presentations of OCD have overt compulsions - compulsions that others can see. If you have observed any of these presentations in yourself, fill them in Worksheet 2 available at the end of this course book and also in the Worksheets workbook, after discussion with your partner.

In the next chapter, we will explore a few more types of OCD of the Pure-O type where compulsions are not visible; where compulsions are mental.

To-Do:
Fill WS2 - presentations of OCD experienced

S1C6. Pure-O OCD

Compulsions such as washing, checking, rearranging, counting and repeating are visible to others. But there are presentations of OCD which have intrusive thoughts or obsessions but no apparent compulsions. This kind of OCD has been called Pure-O OCD. Pure-O is short for purely obsessional. This presentation of OCD was once believed to have only obsessive thoughts and no compulsions (Williams et al, 2013). But this belief is wrong. In some presentations of OCD, compulsions may remain hidden or unidentified, or may be mental in nature (Seyfer, 2021). But compulsions definitely exist. Some of the types of Pure-O OCD are:

Harm OCD: In Harm OCD, the person may believe that he may intentionally or unintentionally cause harm to self or someone else (Moulding et al., 2014). The fear may be about harming to hurt or harming to kill. It could be specific people, random people, kids, or even self. Violent impulses may take the person by surprise and shock at odd times and cause distress. One of the chief fears associated with this type is '*What if I actually cause harm some day?*' or '*What if I am a psychopath?*'

A variation of harm OCD is Hit and Run OCD. The person may feel that he has run someone over with his vehicle and hasn't realized it. This may make him hypervigilant while driving and even the smallest bump on the road may trigger the obsession that he may have hit someone. He may get off the vehicle repeatedly to check, and sometimes, may retrace his path to go back and check to make sure that he hasn't hit anyone (Milliner-Oar et al., 2016).

Death OCD: In this subtype, the person may have an obsessive fear of death, either one's own or someone else's (Kaufman, 2021). The inevitability of death makes dealing with this subtype difficult. Compulsions may include avoiding any and all activities that are perceived as dangerous and could lead to death.

Suicide OCD: This subtype is closely tied to Harm OCD. The person may not want to commit suicide but may persistently battle with the doubt that he may want to and may fear that he may lose control and do it (Vaughn, 2020). Doubts of suicide may make the person avoid heights, sharp objects, chemicals, and anything else that he may think he would willingly use to die.

Religious OCD or Scrupulosity OCD: This subtype affects the believers. They have a strong desire to do right by God. They may begin to fear doing anything wrong that may be considered sinful and may lead to their getting punished (Greenberg & Huppert, 2010). Their obsessions may include immoral thoughts about God or doubts about their faith. Their devotion to God may become their bane.

A variation of Scrupulosity OCD is Secular Scrupulosity OCD or Moral Scrupulosity OCD, which is not governed by religion but a strong sense of right or wrong (Siev et al., 2011). In this presentation, the person may worry about morality or ethics, and may become obsessed with the rights and wrongs. He may find using abusive language incorrect. He may also be unable to lie, or exaggerate, and may also feel the need to confess repeatedly. He could also develop hyper-responsibility and try and set even those things right which may not concern him either too much, or at all.

Sexual Intrusive Thoughts OCD: Intrusive thoughts may take the form of sexual thoughts or sexual images about people, including family members, friends, kids, or even God. This may make the person hate himself for being depraved. Prevalence rate of sexual obsessions in OCD could be between 10.5% and 29.6% with males being more affected than females (Tripathi et al., 2018). There could be various other forms of this type of OCD.

People could obsess about their sexual orientation incest, infidelity, genitalia, sexually abusing adults, animals, children, unborn fetuses, (Palmer et al., 2019 and others), having sex with or kissing strangers, celebrities, touching people inappropriately, imagining people naked, (Lee & Kwon, 2003 and others), having sex with God (Rachman 2007), or changing sexual orientation (Filer & Brockington, 1996).

Somatic OCD (or Sensorimotor OCD): Sensorimotor OCD may involve bodily functions like breathing, swallowing, blinking or staring, and the person may not be able to move his focus away from these sensations (Keuler, 2011). There could be hyper attention towards the bladder, or any other part of the body too. Another aspect of this presentation may be an aversion to surfaces like a chalkboard in anticipation of anxiety caused by 'nails on the chalkboard' feeling.

Peripheral Staring OCD: The person may repeatedly stare at objects in the periphery of his vision. He may not be able to make eye contact and choose to stare elsewhere. OCD may then create an obsession that he wants to stare at the crotch, buttocks or breasts of the opposite person and it may create anxiety, leading to compulsions. This is called Ocular Tourettic OCD. In some cases, people think they may stare but don't. In other cases, people actually, do end up staring (Grayson, & Price, 2021) and making others uncomfortable.

Existential OCD or Philosophical OCD: This is a rare subtype of OCD. The person may become obsessed with existential questions like what is life, what is our purpose on earth, what is the meaning of our existence, and so on (Penzel, 2013). He may try to seek answers to these questions and not finding the answers may cause distress, leading to compulsions.

Guilt OCD or Real Event OCD: People make mistakes and learn to experience remorse, forgive themselves and move on from the episode. A person with Guilt OCD may find it difficult to move on from mistakes committed in the past, sometimes, even from years ago (Farrell, 2021). He may think that the 'crime' that he has committed is not pardonable and often believes that he deserves to be punished for the crime. The rationale that his brain may provide him is that '*While others only think of committing a crime, I already have and I need to be punished for it.*' Accepting that the episode is over and he needs to look ahead, rather than dwell on the past, may become a challenge for him.

Counting OCD: The person may need to count up to a particular number, or do an activity a specific number of times to make the bad thoughts go away. Feeling 'right' is achieved through counting behavior, even though there may be no rationale (VanDalfsen, 2020). For example, a person may need to do certain activities in multiples of four to make sure that the activities have been done right. If done 'wrong,' that is, the activities are not done a specific number of times, like switching the light on and off four times, he may think something bad might happen. At other times, some people may compulsively count everything they can in their environment, a condition called arithmomania (Marais, 2020), which is also an expression of OCD.

Magical Thinking OCD: In the case of magical thinking OCD, obsessions may be about superstitions or magical thinking. The belief may be that events that cannot have a causal relationship may do so (Einstien, & Menzies, 2004). For example, the person may believe that if he steps on cracks in tiles, his wife may die. Or the person may believe superstitions like bad things happening if a black cat crosses his path.

False Memory OCD: This is not a separate sub-type but a different layer of obsession that may develop in any of the subtypes. In False Memory OCD, "people believe that they have experienced an item or event which is actually novel" (Dodson et al., 2000, p. 392). The person may become convinced that the worst has already happened instead of dreading the possibility of it happening. For example, a person with pedophilia OCD may begin to believe that he has indeed molested children (rather than worry about the possibility that he might). He may begin to feel that he may have committed the crime but somehow does not remember it enough to be sure.

Meta OCD: This is another layer over existing presentations of OCD. Sometimes OCD may make a person obsess about his OCD (Wortmann, 2014). So, the person may begin to have doubts like '*Do I really have OCD?*' '*Am I pretending to have OCD?*' '*Am I obsessing about obsessing?*' or even '*Have I been diagnosed properly?*' The doubts move between the actual presentation of OCD and Meta OCD, and if this presentation is not identified, recovery may be affected.

Relationship OCD: In Relationship OCD the obsessions are related to romantic relationships and can be of three types - where you doubt your love for your partner, where you doubt your partner's love for you, and where you doubt if the relationship is 'right' in general (Doron et al., 2012a).

There may be dozens of other presentations or manifestations of the same presentations that may not have been covered here. Awareness is critical because a person may be affected by more than one presentation and understanding what aspects of his life are affected by OCD will help in dealing with OCD in a rounded, holistic way. Before proceeding to the next chapter, discuss with your partner and in Worksheet 2, note down if you are experiencing any of them too.

In the next chapter, we shall understand ROCD better.

To-Do:
Fill WS2 - presentations of OCD experienced

S1C7. Relationship OCD - An introduction

As mentioned, in ROCD the obsessions are related to romantic relationships. ROCD can be of three types - Type 1- where you doubt your love for your partner, Type 2 - where you doubt your partner's love for you, and Type 3 (Doron et al, 2012a) - where you doubt if the relationship is 'right' in general (with elements of the first two types co-existing). These types are numbered only for the sake of convenience in this course book. They are not pre-existing types like Type 1 diabetes and Type 2 diabetes, which are actual classifications.

In ROCD Type 1, that is doubts whether you love your partner or not, obsessions may center on perceived flaws in the partner (Doron et al., 2012b). These flaws may be regarding the partner's intelligence, looks, sense of humor, social skills, competence, or anything that you may consider important. Compulsions may be comparison with other people, checking your own attraction to your partner, or hyper focus on the perceived flaws.

In ROCD Type 2, the obsessions may be about perceived inadequacy in self. These inadequacies may be related to any aspect about you that you may think your partner may dislike you for. Compulsions may be the constant need to check if your partner loves you, or if your partner is cheating on you.

In ROCD Type 3, the obsessions may not be specific to the partner or yourself but about the relationship itself. Doubts if the relationship is right, if it will last, if there is a possibility of a better partner, etc may plague you. Compulsions here may be looking at other couples and wondering if you have what they have, or other rituals around such obsessions.

Importantly enough, not only do people switch from one presentation to another in OCD, but even within ROCD, you may switch types. The presentations may co-exist and even perpetuate one another at times (Szepsenwol et al., 2016). You may start off with ROCD Type 1 and, sometime later you may have an ROCD Type 2 obsession, which is diametrically opposite to ROCD Type 1. This may make you wonder if you have OCD at all. Then it may morph to ROCD Type 3 and add complexity. Sometimes, your anxiety may be on account of not being able to go back to your original presentation. '*Why can't I go back to what it was earlier?*' you may end up remonstrating. So, your ROCD may keep switching from one type to another and may sometimes create obsessions of two types together too.

Hence, being able to differentiate between the types and knowing which type or types of ROCD you are affected by is important too, as the exercises that you will use to deal with them will differ from type to type. We will see this as we go along further in the course book. Discuss with your partner about the types of ROCD you experience and note them down in Worksheet 2.

In the next chapter we shall look at the other forms of ROCD.

To-Do:
Fill WS2 - presentations of OCD experienced

S1C8. Other forms of ROCD

Usually, ROCD is understood to impact only romantic relationships. However, since OCD can morph into just about any form, there are other forms of ROCD that are also observed, that may not be categorized as ROCD, but are in fact, types of ROCD.

ROCD can affect relationships between friends, co-workers, boss-assistant, parent-child (Doron et al., 2017) and even siblings. For example, the doubt that your best friend secretly hates you or does not want to be your friend may be indicative of ROCD. Or, thinking that your boss is trying to find evidence against you to ultimately fire you might be a sign of ROCD. Thinking that your co-workers secretly hate your guts may also be indicative of ROCD.

Thinking that your parents do not love you enough or love your sibling more may also be indicative of ROCD. Thinking that you do not have the best interests of your children in mind and thinking that you are a bad parent, may also be indicative of ROCD. Excessive worrying over whether you are raising your children well or not may be indicative of ROCD too. Thinking that your children hate you may also be indicative of ROCD.

This course book focuses exclusively on ROCD between romantic partners, but knowledge of the other forms may help assess if any of the other symptoms exist and similar techniques as outlined in this course book can be used to deal with those too. Discuss with your partner and fill in any manifestations of ROCD with other relationships in Worksheet 2.

In the next chapter we shall discuss healthy and unhealthy relationships.

To-Do:
Fill WS2 - presentations of OCD experienced

S1C9. Healthy and unhealthy relationships

Relationships are not always healthy. An unhealthy relationship does not necessarily indicate the presence of ROCD. You need to have a correct assessment about your relationship rather than diagnose it as ROCD. If you are in an unhealthy relationship, neither this course book, nor any other book, nor chapter, nor blog, nor podcast on ROCD will be of any use. If you suspect that you have ROCD, get an OCD expert to confirm the diagnosis. Once again, read this chapter with your partner so that both of you can get a better understanding.

Everyone expects that his relationship will be healthy and happy, but unfortunately that is not always the case. Relationships are often unhealthy and sometimes, even abusive. According to estimates, 9% to 38% of young couples could be in unhealthy relationships (González-Ortega et al., 2008) and 35% of women worldwide may have experienced abuse and violence in relationships (World Health Organization, 2017). Through this chapter, I attempt to illustrate the differences to reduce the ambiguity about ROCD.

The relationship spectrum one-page handout, downloadable on www.loveisrespect.org, is a quick-read on the topic. It is available on their website and the link is provided at the end of this chapter. Additionally, www.loveisrespect.org also explains how on parameters such as communication, respect, trust, honesty, equality and personal time, a relationship can be classified as healthy, unhealthy or abusive as shown in figure 1.9.1.

You need to evaluate your relationship at least on these parameters. If you find your partner to be abusive, you may need to end the relationship or seek help. If your relationship is unhealthy, you can work towards improving it by working on the parameters. Many a time, in unhealthy relationships, the abuser is not even aware of his toxic behavior because of being too self-absorbed (Brown, 2017). Hence, observe your own behavior from a third person point of view. If you find yourself guilty of any of the acts listed under unhealthy or abusive relationships, you need to evaluate your choices and seek help if you cannot control them.

In unhealthy and abusive relationships, whatever the abuser does

Figure 1.9.1: The relationship spectrum

Healthy	Unhealthy	Abusive
A healthy relationship means both you and your partner are:	You may be in an unhealthy relationship if your partner is:	Abuse is occurring in a relationship when one partner is:
• Communicating	• Not communicating	• Communicating in a hurtful or threatening way
• Respectful	• Disrespectful	
• Trusting	• Not trusting	• Mistreating
• Honest	• Dishonest	• Accusing the other of cheating when it's untrue
• Equal	• Trying to take control	• Denying their actions are abusive
• Enjoying personal time away from each other	• Only spending time together	
• Making mutual choices	• Pressured into activities	• Controlling
• Economic/financial partners	• Unequal economically	• Isolating their partner from others

to abuse is a choice. The person may not communicate, disrespect, not trust, lie, try to control by choice. In ROCD, however, you may understand that you should not be indulging in these actions but you don't seem to have a choice. In unhealthy or abusive relationships, the abuser may cheat, but in ROCD, you may think you want to but the thought would cause anxiety. In unhealthy and abusive relationships, the dominant feeling may be frustration and anger, and intent to hurt or not care. In ROCD, the dominant feeling may be fear and anxiety, and excessive care.

Conflicts in relationships can be healthy and conflict resolution is a learned skill (Karam et al., 2015). One of the biggest mistakes people make in ROCD is to think that there can be no conflicts and that the relationship should always feel like a fairytale romance. That you should feel loved all the time and that you should feel attracted to your partner all the time. That if you don't feel loved enough by the partner or don't feel enough love towards the partner, there is something wrong.

If you are watching a romantic movie or even porn and if you think of someone else other than your partner, your ROCD brain may immediately latch on to either doubt about the appropriateness of the relationship or guilt about the inappropriateness of the thought. You may feel bad about fantasizing about other people, wishing to spend time with other people or even sharing a joke with other people.

These are just indicative of the differences between unhealthy relationships and ROCD. Make absolutely sure that you have ROCD before you choose to treat it as such. Read the toolkit for healthy relationships for a deeper understanding. Understanding the difference and working actively on areas of improvement can help strengthen a beautiful but shaky relationship.

In the next chapter we shall look at some of the warning signs of ROCD Type 1.

To-Do:
Download the relationship spectrum pdf from https://t.ly/IWQq

S1C10. Warning signs of ROCD - Type 1

Let us look at thirteen telltale signs that may indicate that you have ROCD Type 1. Before that though, here's a word of caution - unless you are clinically diagnosed by a professional, self-diagnosing and assuming that you have ROCD may not be the right thing to do. You may have ROCD, you may have ROCD plus something else, you may have something else altogether or you may have nothing. Practicing what is laid out here will not harm you, but practicing it incorrectly may. Hence, for your own wellbeing, make sure that you are diagnosed by a professional. To figure out if you may have ROCD, Dr. Jordan Levy of NYC compiled a set of thirteen signs for ROCD Type 1. Ask yourself the following questions:

1. Do you test your level of attraction towards your partner by seeing if you are more attracted to other people such as strangers, friends, exes, or celebrities?
2. Are you constantly dwelling over your partner's physical imperfections? For example thinking things like '*Is his/her nose too big or eyebrows too thick/thin?*'
3. Are you constantly picking at your partner's personality? For example, thinking things like '*Is he/she boring? Are his/her jokes too corny? Does he/she feel passionate about all of the same things as me? Is he/she too shy? Is he/she smart enough?*'
4. Do you shy away from dating because no one seems good enough for you?
5. Are you unwilling to take the next step in your relationship because you are focused on his/her flaws or on what is missing in the relationship?
6. Do you constantly feel uncertain about whether or not you are in the 'right' relationship and that maybe there's someone better out there for you?
7. Are you engaged in endless attempts to figure out just how in love you feel with your partner? For example thinking things like '*Why don't I miss him/her more even though we haven't seen each other in over a week? Do I truly feel connected when we are together?*'
8. Do you seek reassurance by comparing your relationship to other relationships? For example thinking things like '*My friend and her boyfriend/girlfriend seem like such a better match than us. They seem so much happier than we are. My parents truly love each*

other and I don't have that. Is it okay if it is not so?'

9. Do you feel like you constantly need reassurance that you have made the 'right' choice in your partner?

10. Are you comparing your relationship to a previous fun and exciting (often unhealthy) relationship to figure out if you feel the same way about your current partner?

11. Are you avoiding watching romantic movies or TV shows that bring up unwanted thoughts and anxiety related to your relationships?

12. Do you persistently look for answers on the internet and online forums?

13. Have you found that sexual activity is a chore and a generally unpleasant and anxiety-filled event?

If you have answered most of these questions as yes, *and* if you feel distressed with these questions, there is a chance that you may have ROCD Type 1. For example, if you feel yourself attracted to someone else more than you are to your partner, instead of considering it as normal attraction, or instead of enjoying the feeling, if you seem to get anxious or feel guilty, to the point of dysfunctionality, it may be an indication that you may have ROCD Type 1.

You will find these questions in Worksheet 3 at the end of this course book and also in the Worksheets file for you to go over and answer for yourself, in consultation with your partner and make a preliminary assessment if you have ROCD Type 1.

In the next chapter, we shall discuss the questions that I have compiled for ROCD Type 2.

To-Do:
Complete WS3 - ROCD - Type 1 traits

S1C11. Warning signs of ROCD - Type 2

Let us now look at the fourteen questions I have compiled for you to determine if you may have ROCD Type 2. I am repeating the note of caution here - unless you are clinically diagnosed by a professional, self-diagnosing and assuming that you have ROCD may not be correct as there may be other reasons affecting your relationships. Hence, make sure you are indeed diagnosed with ROCD by a professional.

If you want to determine whether you have ROCD Type 2 or not, ask yourself these questions:

1. Do you doubt your partner's attraction towards you by checking if she seems happier with other people?
2. Do you worry about your physical imperfections and wonder if your partner may stop loving you because of that? For example thinking things like '*Am I too fat for my partner?*' (Please note that this perceived inadequacy should not be a general inadequacy in your mind but specific to your partner).
3. Do you constantly test your partner's love for you? For example, sending a text and expecting a text back immediately, or saying '*I love you*' just to see if she says it back exactly the way you want to hear it.
4. Do you try to read too much meaning into your partner's words? For example do you keep wondering why she used or did not use specific words while talking to you and whether that means that she does not love you?
5. Do you constantly feel uncertain about whether or not you are in the 'right' relationship and that maybe there's someone better out there for you who would love you the way you wanted?
6. Do you constantly look at other couples and wonder how much in love they seem to be and why your partner cannot behave that way with you?
7. Do you find yourself suspecting everything that your partner says and does? Do you think it is an indication that she is lying to you?
8. Do you seek reassurance from your friends to observe your partner's behavior and confirm to you whether your partner seem to be in love with you or not?
9. Do you constantly question your partner and seek explanations about her behavior? Does your partner feel you have become overbearing?

10. Do you want to go to the next level in your relationship too fast? Do you want your partner to commit to you too soon? Do you feel insecure in your relationship at the current stage?
11. Do you avoid watching romantic movies or TV shows that bring up unwanted thoughts and anxiety related to your relationships?
12. Do you persistently look for answers on the internet and online forums?
13. Do you find yourself stalking your partner's social media profiles to catch her in a lie, even though she has not given you a reason to?
14. Do you think that your partner may find something bad about your past and choose to leave you?

Again, if you have answered most of these questions with a yes, and you constantly have these thoughts on your mind, to the point of dysfunctionality, you may have ROCD Type 2. For example, if you think that your partner may find something bad about your past and may leave you, and if you feel distressed about it, it may be a sign that you have ROCD Type 2. However, ROCD Type 2 may not be a simple thing to diagnose as you cannot determine the real feelings of the other person. Hence, a professional needs to be consulted for the same.

These are not the only signs and there could be various others. But these signs would give you an idea of how ROCD can be detected. These questions have been included in Worksheet 4 at the end of the course book and also in the Worksheets file, which you should look at again along with your partner to determine signs of ROCD Type 2 that you experience.

In the next chapter, we shall take a look at signs that you may have ROCD Type 3.

To-Do:
Complete WS4 - ROCD - Type 2 traits

S1C12. Warning signs of ROCD - Type 3

Let us now look at the questions that I have compiled to help you determine if you have ROCD Type 3, that is relationship focused ROCD. I am reiterating the note of caution that if you are not diagnosed with ROCD by a mental health professional, concluding that you have ROCD merely on the basis of a dysfunctional relationship may not just be incorrect, but also harmful. If you are indeed diagnosed with ROCD, here are some questions you can answer for yourself to determine if you have ROCD Type 3. There are subtle differences and some overlaps between the three types of ROCD. Sometimes, understanding the difference may bring more clarity into the process. Following are the questions you should ask yourself to estimate the presence of ROCD Type 3.

1. Do you doubt your relationship and think that you could be happier with someone else even though there is nothing wrong with your partner?
2. Do you constantly worry about the correctness of committing to your partner despite everything going well?
3. Do you think you may be making a mistake by continuing to be in a relationship with your partner?
4. Do you check if you think of your partner often?
5. Do you constantly find yourself wondering if you think of someone else at romantic moments?
6. Do you keep feeling sometimes that your partner may not be loving enough and hence the relationship may not be sufficient?
7. Do you seek reassurance from your friends about the correctness of your relationship, and you have made the 'right' choice in your partner?
8. Do you avoid watching romantic movies or TV shows that bring up unwanted thoughts and anxiety related to your relationships?
9. Do you persistently look for answers on the internet and online forums?
10. Do you shy away from dating because you don't know what you want from the relationship?
11. Do you compare your relationship to a previous fun and exciting (often unhealthy) relationship to figure out if you feel the same way about your current partner?
12. Do you find that sexual activity is a chore and a generally unpleasant and anxiety-filled event?

If your answer to most of these questions is yes and the responses to these questions are causing anxiety or fear with an urgent need to do something to change the situation, but yet not wanting to, you may have ROCD Type 3. These are not the only signs and there could be various others. But these signs are still a rough indicator of how ROCD can be detected. These questions have been included in Worksheet 5 at the end of the course book and also in the Worksheets file. Take a look at them to discover signs of ROCD Type 3 in your relationship.

This completes the first section. In the next section, we shall look at the factors that affect recovery in ROCD.

To-Do:
Complete WS5 - ROCD - Type 3 traits

Section II: Factors affecting recovery

S2C1. Is there a miracle cure?

I am sorry to be the bearer of bad news, but without beating around the bush, let me tell you that sadly, there is no miracle cure for OCD. But I am certain you know that by now. People often get into extensive research, watching videos, reading blogs and books, listening to podcasts, trying supplements, trying various medicines (self-medication at that), alternative healing methods like Ashwagandha, St John's Worts, Psilocybin or other types of therapeutic interventions such as hypnotherapy, EMDR or even ECT - to find a miracle cure for OCD. They will do everything possible - except ERP.

People self-medicate. On social media forums they ask for names, dosages and other information about medicines that have helped others so that they can take the same. This is not only unhelpful but also dangerous. Unhelpful because the people they talk to are other sufferers and not experts; dangerous because people calibrate the dosage, start and stop medicines as per their whims, and are generally non-compliant. At the whisper of a side effect, they would want to alter the dosage or drop one pill or add another. They do not consider their doctors knowledgeable enough to help them, and end up doing what they think is right.

This is understandable because ERP is the most difficult method to treat ROCD. But whether you like it or not, it is also the most effective. There is really no miracle cure. No amount of reading blogs and books, watching videos and listening to podcasts will help unless you decide to take the recommended action. That is like trying to learn swimming by doing everything but jumping into the pool. It won't help. You will have to jump into the pool. You will have to tolerate the fear of drowning. You are allowed to seek help to learn. You are allowed to even use floats until you are ready to swim on your own. But jumping into the pool is a must. Similarly, jumping into ERP is a must to learn how to manage your ROCD. All things considered, ERP is still the best form of treatment for ROCD. That is the truth, the whole truth and nothing but the truth.

In the next chapter, we shall look at understanding what recovery in ROCD means.

S2C2. Recovery in ROCD

Most people who have OCD, and are yet to understand the premise of recovery want their intrusive thoughts to stop. If you read social media posts of people struggling with OCD, many of them talk about needing the thoughts to stop. According to them recovery would mean no more intrusive thoughts. That is not how recovery works though. Intrusive thoughts will not stop. I'll say this again. Intrusive thoughts will not stop. But, if the recovery process if correctly followed their impact on you will lessen considerably, so that even in their presence, you do not feel too anxious.

For you to consider yourself recovering, you will need to have a friendlier relationship with your anxiety. You will need to understand that some amount of anxiety may forever be your companion. Instead of expecting to be at level zero anxiety, you may need to make peace with the possibility that you may have a low grade (level two or level three) anxiety all the time. *That* may be your new normal.

Intrusive thoughts are a result of the associations that our brains create. The word car may conjure up a different image for me than it might for a small child. That is because my association with the word car is with my black car, whereas a child's association with the word car may be with his favorite toy car. Or the words 'Bread and...' may make someone think of butter, someone of cheese, or someone of jam.

Triggers in OCD are based on the associations created in the mind. So, the association with a romantic movie may bring the thought of being unhappy in the relationship. Hence, a romantic movie that gives rise to the intrusive thought today will definitely give rise to the intrusive thought even after recovery. However, the difference is that today it may be bothersome or even debilitating, whereas tomorrow it may not be. It may become just another thought that you do not attend to.

How does this happen? How does the anxiety go down for the same intrusive thought that causes so much agony today? This happens through the processes of habituation and extinction. Habituation is the process of fear reduction that is the result of a new learning (Benito et al., 2018). When instead of avoiding a trigger, you face it repeatedly the fear associated with it reduces. This is called extinction (Geller et al., 2019).

You get habituated to the situation first through repetition and then the fear goes extinct.

Think of it like this. If you read a funny joke once, it may make you laugh. If you read the same joke again, you may smile, but it won't be as funny as the first time. If you read the same joke five times, it will become boring and unfunny. Because you are habituated to it and repetition has caused desensitization to the humor quotient rendering it extinct.

Similarly, if you watch a horror movie once, you may feel scared. If you watch it again, you will feel a little less scared. If you watch the same horror movie five times, you will begin to get bored. It will not scare you anymore. That stage where an impulse repeated many times stops causing the same feeling as it did the first time is habituation to the situation and extinction of the emotion it evokes. So, if you face your fear repeatedly, it will stop bothering you, because you may begin to get habituated to it or bored of it, and your fear may become extinct.

This works for all types of OCD, including ROCD. Even in ROCD, you may get the thoughts that you do not love your partner enough or that your partner is not right for you even after recovery. But since you would have learnt to handle them better, they would not bother you much. Or at all. Between your partner and yourself, get an understanding of these aspects and realign your expectations from recovery, if they have been different so far.

In the next chapter, we shall look at the factors affecting recovery.

S2C3. Factors affecting recovery

Let us now talk about two factors that majorly affect recovery in ROCD - the severity of the disorder, and the efforts made by the person.

Severity: The first factor is the severity of the disorder. The Y-BOCS test that determines the presence and severity of OCD provides five levels of severity - mild, moderate, severe, very severe, and extreme. A person who has mild ROCD has a better chance of faster recovery than a person who has severe ROCD. The biological influence in a person with severe ROCD is higher than in one with mild ROCD. So, other things being equal, the lesser the severity, the faster the recovery process can work.

Many people assume that the duration for which they have had ROCD will also determine whether they will recover or not. That is however not true. Regardless of the duration for which one has had ROCD, recovery is possible. It may take longer possibly, if you have had ROCD for a long time, because of the psychological inflexibility that may have set in. In the Worksheets file, the Y-BOCS Test (Goodman et al., 1989a, b) has been provided as PT2. Discuss each question with your partner, understand it well, and complete the assessment to know what your level of ROCD is. This is the number that we need to work to bring down.

Efforts: The second and equally important factor on which recovery depends is the effort put in by the person. Recovery in ROCD needs a lot of work. Sometimes the process gets derailed here. Some people may want to put in conditional effort. They may say *'I am willing to work on my ROCD but it should not affect my sleep'*. Or *'I am willing to work on my ROCD but it should not affect my work'*. Or *'I am willing to work on my ROCD but it should not affect my studies'*.

Recovery does not work that way. If you fall in a ditch (something we shall speak about more in the chapter on acceptance), you would not say *'I am willing to work on getting out so long as it does not spoil my clothes.'* You would not bother about your clothes or shoes or hair or anything else. You would prioritize getting out of the ditch over anything else. Similarly, your effort in recovery from ROCD should not be conditional.

Some people say *'We shouldn't have to work on our ROCD. What are the doctors doing? What are we paying them for?'* Well, you are paying them for telling you how to put in the recovery effort. Just as merely paying a swimming instructor will not automatically teach you swimming, or paying a gym instructor will not automatically get you ripped, paying doctors and therapists does not guarantee automatic recovery. You will need to put in the effort of jumping into the pool to learn swimming, working out in the gym to get ripped and practice ERP to get your ROCD under control.

Some people may pretend to work on their ROCD but may not practice ERP well, or at all. ERP is not easy. But if one wants to recover, one needs to continue to work on oneself regardless of how difficult and painful the process is.

These, therefore, are the two factors that affect recovery in ROCD. Care must be taken by the sufferer and his partner to make sure that these issues are borne in mind and addressed adequately.

From the next chapter, we shall start looking at the twelve pillars to recovery in ROCD.

To-Do:
Complete PT2 - Y-BOCS

S2C4. Introduction to the pillars

As indicated, recovery in ROCD is not just a matter of getting medicines, popping pills and being done with it. Recovery from ROCD requires a change - a lifestyle change. I come across many people who do not put any special efforts at learning about the disorder and trying to get better. It is understandable, but not acceptable. Understandable because recovery in ROCD requires changing habits that seem impossible to change. Even for people without ROCD, creating new habits is difficult. With ROCD to stand in the way it is many times more difficult. So, it is understandable.

But it is not acceptable because unless you make specific efforts ROCD may either remain at the same level of severity or end up getting significantly worse, and affect your relationships. Not just the current one, but in case you choose to move on, even the next one and the one after that. As you probably know, the problem is not in your partner, but in your inability to look beyond what your ROCD seems intent to focus on. So, change is important. Recovery would thus require you to adopt a few new habits and break a few old ones.

The first two pillars to recovery are CBT, and ERP. The next five pillars have the acronym MAGIC (mindfulness, acceptance, gratitude, insight, compassion). The next four pillars are diet, sleep, exercise and supplements. The twelfth pillar is medicines. Out of these twelve pillars, this course book will largely focus on the first seven pillars, i.e., CBT, ERP, mindfulness, acceptance, gratitude, insight and compassion.

In the next chapter, we shall explore the concept of CBT.

S2C5. The first pillar - CBT

A question that is frequently asked by many who want to understand how recovery in ROCD works is - what is better for recovery; Cognitive Behavioral Therapy (CBT) or Exposure and Response Prevention (ERP)? Or, sometimes these concepts are used interchangeably. Even by doctors. Many professionals recommend CBT for the treatment of OCD, sufferers go to CBT specialists and come back disappointed and with a firm belief that CBT does not work. Hence, a word of clarification is required. ERP is one of the several types of CBT and is considered to be the gold standard in treatment of all types of OCD (including ROCD; McKay et al., 2015).

So, CBT is an umbrella term, and ERP is a specific branch under this umbrella. As an analogy, CBT is like engineering and ERP is like computer engineering. Just as all computer engineering is engineering but all engineering is not computer engineering, all ERP is CBT, but all CBT is not ERP. In this chapter we shall understand what CBT is.

CBT: CBT has two components to it - *Cognitive* and *Behavioral*. *Cognitive* comes from cognition which refers to thinking. In the *cognitive* part of CBT, the attempt is to change the thinking pattern of the person. The objective is to understand the way the person thinks and identify cognitive distortions (that is thinking errors) to correct faulty thinking (Kuru et al., 2017). For example, if you think that your partner should have all the perfect attributes and no imperfections at all to be worthy of being in a relationship with you, or else the relationship is not ideal, you are a victim of a cognitive distortion referred to as 'All or Nothing' or 'Black or White' thinking. According to the 'All or Nothing' cognitive distortion, your mind tells you that if you do not have everything you want, you cannot be happy.

Through the *cognitive* part of CBT, you are made to understand the irrationality of the thought. Similarly, if your mind tells you that just because your partner has not texted you the way you wanted her to, she is having an affair, it is a cognitive distortion referred to as 'Jumping to Conclusions'. Once you understand the irrationality of your thinking, you can then work towards not falling prey to the cognitive distortions. The *cognitive* part of CBT thus works to realign incorrect thinking.

The *behavioral* part of CBT works towards getting you to change your behavior through a process called cognitive restructuring. For cognitive restructuring, you would need to observe your intrusive and other negative thoughts and map them to the cognitive distortions you identify in each case. Once that is done, you would need to provide an alternate response that is healthier and more adaptive. The next step is to put the restructured cognition into action through implementation.

For example, for the 'All or Nothing' thinking example above, if you restructure your cognition by understanding that it is fine for your partner to not have all perfect attributes, the behavioral change you bring about is accepting the imperfections in your partner. Or in the 'Jumping to Conclusions' example above, if you restructure your cognition by realizing that your jumping to conclusions is erroneous, you may be able to stop yourself behaviorally from confronting your partner about the ostensible affair that she might be having.

If CBT is not administered and the understanding of the irrationality of the thought is not provided, modifying behavior is possible but the effort may seem unreasonable and hence difficult.

The entire next chapter focuses on these cognitive distortions. Read through them many times and absorb the information well. Try to map your obsessions and other thoughts to the cognitive distortions to understand their irrationality. The more aware you are, the better you will get at handling your irrational thoughts. Your grasp of them should be strong enough for you to be able to explain them to a small child, if needed.

S2C6. Cognitive distortions

As discussed in the previous chapter, cognitive distortions are thought patterns that may convince us of things that are not necessarily true or correct. Since our mental well being depends upon the thoughts that cross our minds, these distortions can cause severe damage in case of negative thought patterns. We may keep feeling that we are right in our assessment of the situation, may make incorrect decisions, may take incorrect actions, and may end up making either ourselves, or others, or both, miserable.

Some cognitive distortions may impact us more than others and sometimes more than one distortion may be present at the same time. Recognizing that you are a victim to these cognitive distortions may enable you to deal with the situation in a more rational way. It may sometimes be instrumental in helping you salvage your breaking or broken relationships, as well as lifting your own sense of self-esteem.

Cognitive distortions are also very sneaky. They make their way into our lives and take over our thinking so sneakily that sometimes we do not even realize when we become the victims to these distortions until they are pointed out to us. More awareness and internalization of these distortions and modifying behavior through cognitive restructuring will make our thinking more adaptive and speed up the recovery process. We shall touch upon twelve cognitive distortions, recognizing them and learning how to counter them.

1. Filtering: As the name suggests, filtering refers to leaving out something – in this case, the positives. Like using a camera filter that allows light of a specific kind and filters out what is unneeded. Filtering, as a cognitive distortion, refers to developing a blinkered view of what one sees and leaving out what goes against the view that one has formed. For example, whenever your partner does not text on time, you may notice it, but when she does, you may not. This means you may be filtering out all the times she does text you on time and may believe that she never texts back on time, which causes you to become anxious.

For cognitive restructuring in this distortion, you need to closely look at all these situations and objectively see both sides of the coin. You can ask yourself if what you are feeling is really absolutely true or there are points that you have been ignoring. What is the evidence in favor of your thinking and what is the evidence against? Is there a different way of looking at things or is yours the only way? Are you looking at the situation through a negative filter? If so, only the negatives will pass through and the positives will be left out. When you learn to look at the situation from a rounded perspective rather than at an episodic level, you may be able to see more clearly and reject the filtered thinking for a more appropriate view.

2. Black or white thinking: Life is never either black or white. There are various shades of grey in between and all our situations, achievements, objectives, goals and so on may fall somewhere on this spectrum. But a person with this distortion may sometimes fail to understand this. So, he is either perfect, or a complete failure. There is no in-between. Thus, if your mind tells you that you should either have a complete fairytale romance or not at all, you may be disregarding a good relationship just because there may be some struggle that you may be going through. Or, if your mind says that either your partner is perfect in all attributes or your partner is no good, you may be disregarding what you are getting for what you are not.

You may need to develop a realistic view in life for cognitive restructuring in this distortion. If you work on the premise that you are perfect and deserve perfection, you may be allowing this distortion to win. Your ROCD may make you feel that you are the centre of the universe and deserve nothing but the best. But you may need to realize that you have your own flaws and are yet accepted by your partner. You may need to develop the attitude of being willing to give more than you get.

Conversely, if you think you have to be perfect and you are not allowed to make any mistakes, you may be a victim of this distortion too. If however, you realize that it is alright, and even healthy, for you to be imperfect and to make mistakes sometimes, you may be able to release yourself from this cage that you have trapped yourself into. The pressure to either always be perfect or else have low self-worth will be lifted and you may be able to accept yourself a lot more.

3. Overgeneralization: Based on one bad experience with a girl, if someone decides that all women are cheats and undependable, he may be a victim of the cognitive distortion of overgeneralizing. He may not be making allowance for the fact that other girls may not be that way. This may lead to disappointment and resentment and possible shutting down of avenues which he could have explored.

Or if after a breakup someone says *'it happens only with me – I never catch a good break'*, he may have fallen prey to overgeneralization as well. He may not be open to the idea that her generalization is not true. Particularly in ROCD, if you think that your partner always reaches for your dates late, or never compliments you, you may be overgeneralizing.

In this case, you may need to look at the situation mindfully and arrive at a more accurate perspective. Is it really true that *all* women are undependable? Or is it possible that there are some women who are loyal and truthful as well? Is it also true that there are some men who are cheats and undependable too? Would it be fair to brand all men as cheats, in that case? Also, is it true that it *always* happens *only* with me? Or have there been times when I have actually had good breaks? Have I not seen others having bad breaks? Is such an absolute statement actually true? Finally, is it really true that my partner always reaches late or never compliments me or am I exaggerating and overgeneralizing? An accurate assessment of these absolute statements may help us realign our thinking to a more correct position.

4. Jumping to conclusions: When we end up making decisions without considering all possibilities or all variables we may be victims of the cognitive distortion called jumping to conclusions. There may not be sufficient evidence to prove the conclusion that we may have arrived at. This distortion often manifests itself in one of two types – mind reading or future seeing.

For example, if you make a grammatical mistake while you are with your partner's friends, you may end up thinking – everyone must be laughing at me behind my back, thinking *'What a doofus I am and my partner thinks less of me because of it'*, it would be an example of mind reading. If this makes you think that your partner may break up with you because of a mistake like that, it would be an example of future seeing.

Since these thoughts may lead to an estimation of whether your relationship will succeed or fail and determine your actions, it would be wise to challenge these negative thoughts. You may once again, need to take stock of all the evidence you have.

In the case of mind reading, you may ask yourself questions like *'Am I the only one who has ever made a grammatical mistake? Was the mistake so terrible that it would make people laugh at me? Do I have any evidence that people are laughing at me? Do I have evidence that my partner thinks less of me because of this?'* In the case of future seeing, you could ask yourself *'Is my mistake really reason enough for my partner to break up with me? Do I have any evidence at all that my feeling will necessarily come true?'* Getting correct responses to these questions may help you in dealing with this cognitive distortion better.

5. Catastrophizing: Catastrophizing is taking a minor incident and blowing it out of proportion – imagining the worst possible outcome where any number of possibilities may exist. For example, if your partner has not invited you to an office party, instead of considering the possibility that it may not be a couples' event, you may choose to believe that people at your partner's office do not like you, and they may be poisoning your partner's mind against you, as a result of which your partner may lose interest in you and break up with you. This may lead you to feel depressed about yourself.

To deal with this, ask yourself this simple question *'Even though what I think is a possibility, what really is the probability that it will actually come true?'* You may realize, again when you put all the evidence together, that even though the possibility exists, the probability of something like that coming true is minuscule. There could be several reasons why your partner did not take you to the office party, and not being liked by his colleagues may not even come close to the real reason. So is the assumption that you are making even remotely true?

6. Personalization: Personalization is when you think that you are totally or partially responsible for everything bad that happens around you, including acts of God. For example if your partner is in a foul mood, you may believe that it may be because of something you have done. Your mind may not allow you to consider the possibility that your partner's bad mood may be because of an argument at work and may have nothing to do with you.

Once again, this is a result of not looking at the various possibilities and only choosing to pick the one that causes the most anxiety. When you are a little more mindful of the other possibilities and choose not to dwell on that one possibility that seems real, despite lack of evidence, you may be able to better handle the distortion.

7. Control fallacy: Control fallacy refers to the distorted thinking related to control. It may manifest in two ways. You may have the feeling that you control situations around you and hence are responsible or the feeling that you are not able to control situations at all. You may disregard the importance of external factors in any event. For example, thinking that you (and only you) are responsible for your partner's happiness is a control fallacy. So, you may do everything you think will make your partner happy, and may make her feel smothered.

On the flip side, thinking that only your partner is responsible for your happiness or that your partner is responsible only for your happiness is also control fallacy. In case someone cheats on his partner, or is abusive towards his partner and states that if she had taken more steps to keep him happy, he would not have acted that way, it is a control fallacy. Insight is important in identification of control fallacy and disallowing it to govern your decisions and actions.

8. Fallacy of fairness: When you feel that the world is not being fair to you, even though you have given your best to the world, you may be experiencing this cognitive distortion. This distortion may make you feel that it is only right that you should be treated better than you think you are. When that does not happen, it may upset you.

For example, if I lend you an umbrella when it is raining and you don't have one, I may automatically begin to assume that when I don't have an umbrella, you will lend me one. If you don't lend me an umbrella when I need one, I may be disappointed. As the saying goes – expecting the world to be nice to you just because you are nice is like expecting a lion to not eat you because you are vegetarian. The world will not always dance to my tunes. If I want to avoid disappointment, I need to recognize that.

In the case of ROCD, if you feel the need to confess to your partner every time you see an attractive girl, and get upset that your partner does not confess to you every time she sees an attractive male, the fallacy of fairness may be governing your thoughts. In such cases, recognizing that it is not necessary for your partner to have the same habits as you, and allowing her to be comfortable in her own ways will help you deal with the fallacy of fairness.

9. Blaming: When we choose not to own up for something that goes wrong and shift responsibility on to others, we refer to it as blaming. We could blame either some other person, or some situation. For example, if you skip a class and go for a movie with your partner and tell her that she made you miss your class because of the movie, you are blaming her. What you need to acknowledge is that you went for the movie with your partner because you wanted to. You knew very well that the class will be missed. You did not want to risk your partner going for the movie with another man. Hence blaming her is unfair to her.

We have control over our actions and we need to take responsibility for them. We are not responsible for anyone else's happiness, but conversely, no one else is important for ours either. The responsibility lies squarely on our shoulders. The sooner we recognize it, the better we will be able to deal with this.

10. Shoulds: Also called 'rigid rule keeping', this is a situation when we have a list of rules about the way things should be. If things aren't the way we want them to be, it affects us. If we have these rules for ourselves, it upsets us, if we break any of them. When we create rules for ourselves and for others that do not have a basis in logic, but are more out of stubbornness, we may end up making ourselves miserable or angry when the rules are not followed.

For example, if you believe that your partner *should* want to spend all her free time with you, or if you believe that you *should* not be thinking about other girls when you are with your partner, you are engaging in rigid rule keeping. Understanding that the words 'should', 'must', 'ought to', and 'have to' constrain us and make us rigid, can help us deal with this distortion better.

11. Emotional reasoning: 'I feel it, therefore it must be true'. When we are not able to separate fact from feeling and think that whatever we feel is actually true, we may let emotional reasoning get the better of us. If you feel that your partner may leave you for some other man, despite knowing that she loves you and is loyal to you, you may be allowing emotional reasoning to cloud your judgment. The feeling here is that your partner may leave you. The fact is that you know she will not leave you. But you choose to let the feeling decide the course of action and not the facts of the situation. The solution to this distortion is to be mindful about separating fact from feeling and be able to operate from the fact mindset, rather than the feeling mindset.

12. Fallacy of change: When we think that if we pressurize people enough, or cajole them enough, they will change and see our point of view, we are engaging in the fallacy of change. Sometimes persuasion works.

But at other times, it may backfire. We hear of instances when girls beg their boyfriends to not leave them, or vice versa. Or when they have already been dumped, beg them to come back. When the ex-partner doesn't relent, the affected person finds it difficult to handle the rejection. The affected person may want to change the ex-partner's mind for what she thinks is the right reason, but the ex-partner may not look at it that way.

At some level, most people may be aware of some cognitive distortions at play in their lives, even if they can't name them. They may still be unable to change themselves. So if changing yourself is so difficult, imagine how successful you would be at trying to change someone else. Trying to change the other person's views by forcing her to necessarily see things from your point of view may have the opposite effect. Realizing this may help you have a better view of the situation. You can learn to temper your persuasive ways with space, or after a point, give up your coercive ways.

As can be seen, sometimes multiple cognitive distortions work together to contort our worldviews for us. In the interest of our own mental wellbeing, it is important to know about these distortions and make sure that they are properly identified, dealt with, and eliminated.

In the Worksheets file and the Worksheets section at the end of this course book, you will find Worksheet 6 on Cognitive Restructuring. Fill it in regularly as a way of restructuring your thinking as a habit and you will find your cognition changing over a period of time.

In the next chapter, we shall understand the concept of ERP.

To-Do:
Complete WS6 - cognitive restructuring

S2C7. The second pillar - ERP

The second pillar of recovery is ERP. ERP stands for exposure and response prevention. It is also sometimes referred to as Exposure and Ritual Prevention and/or notated as Ex/RP, and there is really no difference in the two. For the purpose of this course book, we shall refer to it as ERP. ERP is still the treatment of choice for all forms of OCD, including ROCD, as it is evidence based and effective (Khodarahimi, 2009) and is associated with a long-term remission rate of 32% to 70% (Burchi et al., 2018). ERP has two key terms - exposure and response prevention.

Exposure involves getting exposed by choice to the triggering events for the purpose of triggering the obsessive thoughts. Why in the world would anyone want to get exposed to his triggers by choice? It is bad enough, as it is that you get exposed to them all day anyway, right? Wrong!

There is a strong purpose in getting exposed to your triggers deliberately. The purpose is to desensitize oneself to the fear by facing it continuously. The purpose is to render the fear extinct, through habituation. Like the analogy of a horror movie not remaining scary after being watched repeatedly, your triggers will also lose their edge if faced repeatedly. But - you need to face your fears and *not* do the compulsions that your mind asks you to do in the moment.

For example, you may choose to expose yourself to the anxiety by watching a romantic movie. This may give rise to obsessions, which may give rise to the urge to do the compulsions. You may want to stop watching the movie. You may want to compare physical attributes. You may get the urge to neutralize the thoughts, by telling yourself that your partner's nose is not too long. Or, you may get the urge to seek reassurance from others if your partner looks good.

These compulsions are the usual responses you provide to your obsessions. The response prevention portion of ERP requires you to *not* counter an obsessive thought with the usual compulsive response. In this case, for example, since the compulsive urge is to stop watching the movie, you would continue to watch the movie. Since the compulsion is to compare physical attributes, you would learn how not to do it. You would learn to not neutralize your thoughts or seek reassurance from others about this. In short, you would learn to not do your compulsions as a response to your obsessions and wait for the anxiety to go down on its own.

You may wonder why you would feel less anxious if you don't do the compulsion. Wouldn't your anxiety actually rise? The reason is fairly simple to understand, but difficult to implement. Think of an alcoholic who wants to give up drinking. When he tries to give up drinking and stays away from alcohol, his body demands alcohol, as the body is used to having alcohol in the system. The body will protest and he will have withdrawal symptoms like headache, nausea, anxiety or even hallucinations. He will have an intolerable craving of alcohol.

But eventually, if he resists it long enough, despite the increasing urges, the need for the alcohol begins to diminish and soon, he does not feel the need to drink any longer. Similarly, in the case of ROCD, not doing the compulsion may increase the anxiety in the beginning. But if the compulsions are resisted, the anxiety will eventually subside by itself.

Also think of learning a new skill. When you first want to learn driving, and you sit behind the wheel, there is fear - of losing control of the vehicle, getting into an accident, hurting people, and damaging property. All these are valid concerns. Yet, if you decide not to get behind the wheel to learn driving, you will never overcome the fear. However, if you persist in spite of the fear, you not only get better at driving, but you also begin to lose the fear, as you get habituated to it by facing it often enough.

Can you think of other examples where you did not know how to do something in the beginning, were bad at it, but with repeated practice, you got better at it? Hint – your childhood. Even activities like brushing your teeth followed that process. There was no fear, but there was difficulty, which you managed and at which you got better. At the end of this course book and also in the Worksheets file, you will find Worksheet 7. Fill it in to understand how capable you are at learning new things.

The idea behind filling this worksheet is for you to recognize once again that if you put your mind at something, you can achieve it. You may not master it, but through repetition you can do it well enough to put it on your resume. The same principle works with anxiety. If we face the obsession without doing the compulsion the anxiety goes up in the beginning. But after some time, through repeat exposure, the anxiety begins to fall. It is almost as if your ROCD gives up on you because you are not giving in.

The process of recovery through ERP seems difficult, and it is. But what is expected of you is not superhuman strength. You are not expected to handle snakes or walk on fire. You are merely expected to replicate the average action of average people.

If you pick out one hundred people at random either on the street or out of the telephone directory and question them on their relationship behavior, you will have an understanding of what average relationship behavior is. This course book will expect you to be able to replicate that average behavior. Nothing more, nothing less.

In the next chapter, I shall be discussing the third pillar of recovery in ROCD, and the first one of the MAGIC acronym, which is mindfulness.

To-Do:
Fill WS7 - things you got good at with practice

S2C8. The third pillar - Mindfulness

When you hear the word mindfulness, what image do you see in your mind? Most people when they hear the word visualize the Buddha sitting in a lotus position with his eyes closed, and some oriental pipe-music (generally a flute) playing in the background. They also believe that practicing mindfulness means focusing on their breathing. Do you believe that too? If you do, you are both right and wrong. Mindfulness is a grossly misunderstood concept, not unlike many other concepts in psychology. This chapter is not sufficient to cover everything there is to know about mindfulness, so, I am going to try to crunch the information for you in a more digestible package.

Simply put, mindfulness is focusing your attention in a non-judgmental or accepting way on the experience occurring in the present moment (Kabat-Zinn, 1994). It is an awareness of the present moment experience with acceptance (Germer et al., 2005). Mindfulness is the state of being able to focus on the task at hand with attention and awareness, without letting other factors cause a distraction i.e., present moment awareness (Behan, 2020). This is to be achieved non-judgmentally, non-critically. Let me explain the individual components.

First, mindfulness is about being in the present moment - having present-moment awareness. Where does your mind reside? In the past, regretting mistakes, feeling guilty, longing for things that are over? Or, does it reside in the future, worrying about things that have not happened yet and may never happen? Or does your mind truly reside in the present, focusing only on the current task with complete dedication? If your mind resides anywhere but in the present moment, and you do not recognize it enough to bring it back to the present, you are not being mindful.

The second component is to stay in the present moment non-judgmentally. Being non-judgmental means not assigning a quality to the task at hand. Thinking that a task is unpleasant will make you want to hurry up and finish it, so that you can focus on a more pleasant task. When you do that, you are not being mindful. And mindfulness involves doing this activity non-critically. If you are trying to focus on an activity, your mind will wander and because you know you need to bring it back to the present moment, you may try to do it. But the mind will wander a hundred times. Eventually, you may get frustrated and be critical of yourself that you are not able to be mindful. The quest for being mindful will become something which you think you fail at, and become self-critical.

Know that your mind will wander and know that mindfulness is not about staying focused the entire time. Mindfulness is about recognizing when you are defocusing and bringing yourself back. Thus, mindfulness is the practice of trying to stay in the present moment and focusing on the current task with a non-judgmental and non-critical attitude. Mindfulness is reminding yourself that your thoughts are straying from the current task. Mindfulness is bringing your thoughts back gently to the current task when you see them wandering.

There is a psychometric test provided as PT3 in the Worksheets file - the Mindfulness Attention Awareness Scale (Brown, & Ryan, 2003). "The trait MAAS is a 15-item scale designed to assess a core characteristic of mindfulness, namely, a receptive state of mind in which attention, informed by a sensitive awareness of what is occurring in the present, simply observes what is taking place" (Brown, & Ryan, 2003). Take the test to note your mindfulness. Higher the score, the better you are at being mindful. The practice of mindfulness is very critical to recovery too, which we shall see in the next section.

In the next chapter, I am going to elaborate on the attitudinal foundations of mindfulness.

To-Do:
Complete PT3 - MAAS

S2C9. Attitudinal foundations of mindfulness

Jon Kabat-Zinn, the foremost authority in mindfulness and the developer of the Mindfulness Based Stress Reduction (MBSR) program gives us the seven attitudinal foundations of mindfulness. The seven foundations are non-judgmental attitude, patience, beginner's mind, trust, non-striving attitude, acceptance, and the attitude of letting go or non-attachment (Kabat-Zinn, 2013). I shall also briefly discuss how you can use them to deal with your ROCD. The seven attitudinal foundations of mindfulness are as below:

1. Non-Judgmental Attitude: Mindfulness requires you to have a non-judgmental attitude towards your thoughts. When you practice mindfulness, you may begin to notice that your mind is being judgmental. You may have thoughts such as *'this is boring', 'I can't do this', 'I am bad at this'*, and so on. The objective of mindfulness is not to try to stop the judgment, but just observe that it is occurring and notice how you feel about it.

For example, when you do a mundane chore like washing the dishes, you may feel bored and may either not want to do it at all or do them hastily to get it done with. In that moment, if you are aware that you are feeling bored, and your mind wanders, you can try to bring it to the present moment and focus on doing the job better. In the context of your ROCD, when you have an obsessive thought, notice if you find yourself saying, 'this is a bad thought' or 'this is a scary thought'. When you notice it, try to shed the judgment and make an attempt to classify it as just another ROCD thought (neither good nor bad).

2. Patience: When you learn to practice mindfulness, you need to learn the valuable art of patience. There are no magic pills in recovery and the process takes time as it is a new skill you are learning. Your brain needs to develop the habit of doing the right thing and that will be possible only through practice. Whether it is ERP that you are practicing or mindfulness itself, the key to mastery is repetition and patience. You may make mistakes and you may often fail in your objective. But with patience, you will begin to get better at the practice.

For example, if you want to learn juggling, it will require a lot of patience on your part. Unless you are gifted, you may not be able to learn juggling without patience and repeat practice. In the context of your ROCD thoughts, have the patience to recognize that you will take time to accept the thoughts without needing to do your compulsions. Learn to resist your compulsions repeatedly to overcome ROCD.

3. Beginner's Mind: Mindfulness also requires you to learn to have a beginner's mind. When you engage in some routine activity, you work on auto-pilot and allow your mind to wander, without actually noticing the details. For example, you may not be able to recollect the pattern of the wallpaper in your house without needing to look at it again, as you may not have observed it very closely. However, when you notice or do something new, your mind may be more focused on the task.

For example, if you have never seen a mobile phone before and one is handed to you, you may look at it with curiosity and attention. This curiosity and attention is referred to as the beginner's mind and is an important attitude for mindfulness. It allows you to fully absorb what is happening at that moment. It is as if you are looking at something with the eyes of an alien who finds the experience new.

In the context of your ROCD, when you have an obsessive thought, you can activate the beginner's mind and ask yourself mindfully - what am I experiencing as I am getting this thought? Observe the fear, observe the discomfort. Observe the push of the obsessions and the urgency to do the compulsions. Learn what to pay attention to, and learn what to let go of.

4. Trust: An important foundation of mindfulness is trust - the trust that you build in yourself. Trust that tells you that you can handle this situation yourself and do not need external crutches. You need to look into yourself when a situation arises. You interrogate yourself. You determine the validity of the thoughts and feelings yourself. You learn to break away from the thoughts yourself.

If you get the thoughts that your relationship is not the best, you recognize the thoughts for what they are - just stray thoughts. You recognize that these thoughts are being fed to you by someone else, namely your ROCD. You learn that even though the thoughts originate in your brain, it is indeed another entity that is responsible, and not the core you. You learn to delink from the thoughts and do not integrate them into your reality. When you trust yourself, you are able to do this yourself without seeking any external reassurance about the rightness of your relationship.

You do not need your thoughts to be validated by others. Instead of believing what your ROCD tells you blindly, you trust your core self to do the right thing.

5. Non-Striving Mind: The next important attitudinal foundation in the practice of mindfulness is of the ability of being non-striving. Being non-striving means not attaching your efforts to an immediate outcome. Being non-striving means putting in the efforts towards a goal but not being in a rush to measure progress with each step taken. Sometimes it may seem like there is no progress being made but you continue to put in the efforts because that is the right thing to do.

For example, if you have a baby at home, you feed the baby and give it right care. But every time you feed the baby, you do not measure its height or weight and be disappointed if there is no change. Even if there is no visible change, you do not give up. You do not stop feeding the baby. The goal is to turn the baby into a strong grown up, which you realize will not be achieved in a day. Thus, you care for the baby in a non-striving manner, and eventually, you begin to see the baby growing up.

In the context of your ROCD, when you practice ERP, you may try to do so with the intention of relieving your anxiety immediately. But that is a state of striving. It may prove to be counterproductive when despite trying your best your anxiety does not go down. But if you practice response prevention without attaching the goal of immediate gratification to it, you will get better at it and eventually your efforts will start showing results.

6. Acceptance: Acceptance is one of the pillars to recovery which we shall be exploring in the next chapter as well. However, acceptance is also one of the attitudinal foundations of mindfulness and deserves mention here. Acceptance is a state of no-resistance, when you do not want to change anything. When you want to change something, you may not be accepting it. You may be resisting it. You may be in denial about the situation. Acceptance is also not being resigned to the situation. That may still indicate the need to change it, but inability to do so. Acceptance is the understanding that the situation is the way it is and that if you do not resist it, deny it or resign to it, you may become happier.

Acceptance does not however mean being resigned to the situation. With complete acceptance, though, you can build the commitment to make a change for the better. If I accept my situation, I do not waste my faculties over ruing it or feeling sadness or guilt or frustration. I recognize it for what the situation is and focus on what I can do to emerge from it. Not accepting the situation would compromise my ability to tackle it well.

In the context of your ROCD, when you get an obsessive thought, you accept it by recognizing that you have ROCD. Accept that it has happened often in the past, it has happened again, and it will happen in future too. Acceptance of the thought will prepare you for the next step - to effectively resist your compulsions.

7. Non-attachment: There may be many moments in our lives that we may want to hold on to. Pleasant thoughts, feelings, memories, we choose to hold on to more. But if there are unpleasant thoughts, feelings, experiences or memories, we want to get rid of them as they cause distress. Developing the attitude of non-attachment is important to becoming more mindful. Non-attachment refers to observing the experience every moment without assigning it meaning and without either clinging to it or shunning it. Reinhold Niebuhr summed it up beautifully in the serenity prayer - *Father, give us courage to change what must be altered, serenity to accept what cannot be helped, and the insight to know the one from the other.*

In the context of ROCD, non-attachment refers to understanding that if there is a distressing obsessive thought, it will pass too. So will the relief experienced after doing the compulsion. In a state of non-attachment, you may not shun the obsessive thought or crave the satisfaction of having done the compulsion.

These are the attitudinal foundations to mindfulness and how they relate to your ROCD. Table 2.9.1 gives a quick look of how these foundations relate to your ROCD. Be sure to refer to it when you have obsessive thoughts and want to mindfully deal with them.

Table 2.9.1: Attitudinal Foundations with ROCD

Attitude	Response to Obsession
Non-Judgment	'Hmm, this is another obsessive thought that I am getting' (neither good nor bad)
Patience	'This will take time to go; it will not go away immediately'
Beginner's Mind	'What am I experiencing in my thoughts? What am I experiencing in my body?'

Trust	'I can handle this myself. I do not need reassurance from others on this'
Non-Striving Mind	'Let me not pressurize myself to be rid of this immediately; let me do what I can'
Acceptance	'This happens often, this has happened again, this will happen again in future'
Non-Attachment	'This will pass too, let me not hold on to it'

In the next chapter, we shall look at an exercise to build more awareness of the present moment.

To-Do:
Practice mindfulness with your obsessions

S2C10. Building awareness

The MAAS assesses two aspects of mindfulness - your attention and your. Following is a simple exercise to develop better awareness to improve attention.

Exercise to build awareness:

1. Set alarms on your mobile phones at one hour intervals from the moment you wake up to the time you retire for the day.
2. When an alarm rings, observe your thoughts. Are your actions and thoughts in alignment? Or are you doing one thing and thinking about another? For example, are you washing dishes and thinking about your date in the evening? Are you eating and worrying about a meeting? If you are, you can bring back your thoughts to the present moment.
3. For every hour, fill in Worksheet 8 provided at the end of this course book and also in the Worksheets file. Every time you are mindful, write Y and every time you are unmindful, write N in the appropriate space. In the beginning, you may observe more N entries than Y. But as you become more aware, the number of N's should decrease and the number of Y's should increase.
4. As days go by and awareness gets stronger, switch pattern from one-hour alarms to alarms at random times. Keep noticing where your thoughts are when the alarm rings.

By the end of the month, if you follow through the exercise diligently, you will become far more aware of your thoughts and will have moved towards better awareness.

In the next chapter, we shall explore one of the relaxation exercises that help in building the mindfulness muscle - progressive muscle relaxation (PMR).

To-Do:
Fill WS8 - developing awareness

S2C11. Progressive muscle relaxation

When your brain perceives danger, it responds with a 'stress response' and you feel anxious. Engaging in relaxation exercises may help you deal with your anxiety and you may feel calmer. There are various types of relaxation techniques that can be adopted to achieve calm. When systematic desensitization was first conceptualized, relaxation exercises were included in ERP (Wolpe, 1954) and are still used frequently (Whiteside et al., 2016).

One of the ways in which you can teach your body to relax is progressive muscle relaxation. When you are anxious, one of the physical manifestations is tensing of muscles. When your muscles relax, the tension in them eases off and you feel calmer. Using PMR, you can release the tension in your muscles to relieve the feelings of anxiety.

In PMR, you are required to tense a group of muscles as you breathe in through movements like clenching or flexing, and relax them as you breathe out. All the muscles are systematically worked upon in a certain order, starting with the toes and progressively moving up, covering other muscles, until all the muscles in the body are relaxed.

Also, PMR may help you sleep better if you have trouble falling asleep. If you practice PMR for at least a week to ten days before you start the process of facing your fears, you can get better at the skill of relaxing yourself when stressed and that will be a helpful skill to have after exposures.

PMR should be practiced as a discipline by both you and your partner and not just for the duration of the recovery process. It is a skill that can come handy anytime even in the future, whether or not you are battling with your ROCD. You do not even need to know how to do it yourself. There are various guided meditation apps like Calm, Insight Timer, Headspace, etc that provide you with audios that you need to listen to and just follow the instructions provided. Once you get better at it, you may not need to listen to the audio and you may be able to do PMR at will from memory. But even if you always need to use a guided meditation audio or video for PMR, it is fine.

To start PMR, choose a place where, and time when there will be no interruptions (such as the TV blaring or the kids screaming or the dog barking and so on) and lie down on your back and make yourself comfortable. Breathe slowly and deeply four or five times and focus on your breath. Breathe in slowly as if smelling a rose and breathe out slowly as if blowing a balloon. Deep and slow breathing helps the brain to calm down.

Start PMR by tensing your toes while breathing in for about 5 seconds. As you breathe out, relax the toes. Move to your other muscles after that and follow the same process. Move up to your calves, your thighs, and so on. Doing this for the muscles of the entire body will have a relaxing effect. You may begin to notice that your muscles feel completely relaxed and your stress reducing after following this method.

After you have completed your PMR, breathe in and out slowly and deeply once again for five times and complete the exercise. The whole exercise should not take more than fifteen minutes at the most.

When you do the PMR regularly, every morning and evening and whenever you have an extra fifteen minutes, you will get into the practice and then will be able to use it when you are feeling anxious. It is important to build the practice of PMR on a regular basis. You need to do it enough number of times when you are not anxious for you to be able to use it when you are. Trying to use PMR to calm yourself down when you are anxious without building sufficient practice is like trying to repair a leaking roof when it is raining. If you repair it when it is not raining, it is likely to hold better.

At the end of this course book, in the PMR sheet provided as Additional Resource 2, you will find links to two YouTube videos, one in a male voice and the other in a female voice. Use whichever you are comfortable with. You will also find a list of the muscle groups with suggestions on how to tense and un-tense them, that has been taken from an article from the University of Michigan Health website. If you use PMR regularly, you can train yourself to relax in the most stressful of situations.

In the next chapter, we shall look at the next pillar of recovery, which is acceptance.

To-Do:
Read AR2 - Progressive Muscle Relaxation (PMR)
Practice PMR

S2C12. The fourth pillar - Acceptance

What exactly is acceptance? When I pose this question to people, some of them feel that they have accepted their ROCD. Upon probing, it emerges that they do not accept it, but they acknowledge its presence grudgingly and allow it to pull them down. It is more a sense of resignation than a position of true acceptance. It is more like, *'What can I do? I have it now and I have to live with it.'* Or, *'I know I have ROCD, and it sucks. I want to be rid of it so that I can live my life well'*. Statements like that may be acknowledgment but not true acceptance. It places a burden on the person to get well before he can start fulfilling his dreams.

So, what is true acceptance? How is it even possible to accept a mental disorder, especially one so debilitating as ROCD? True acceptance is when you say *'Yes I know I have ROCD and I am okay with it. I will work to do my best despite it'*. Being okay with ROCD does not mean you will not work towards getting better. You will however work from a better frame of mind - one of strength rather than weakness. In other words, acceptance means "taking a stance of non-judgmental awareness and actively embracing the experience of thoughts, feelings, and bodily sensations as they occur" (Hayes et al., 2004).

Say, you are trekking in a forest. Unmindfully, you fall into a pit dug up for trapping animals. You do not keep wallowing that you have fallen into the pit and that there is no hope for you. You accept that you have a problem and try your best to come out of the ditch. Let us see what all you are truly accepting in a situation like that, and juxtapose that understanding with your ROCD thoughts, as shown in table 2.12.1.

Table 2.12.1: Acceptance Comparison Illustration

No	Falling in a pit	Having ROCD
1	You are in a pit.	You have ROCD
2	You are going to be delayed	You may take time to achieve your dreams
3	You have to try to come out	You have to try to get better
4	You need to want to come out	You need to want to get better
5	You can come out.	You can get better
6	You may have to seek help	You will have to use the 12 pillars

7	The process of coming out is difficult	The process of recovery is difficult
8	The process of coming out is worth it	The process of recovery is worth it
9	You will reach point B, but later	You will achieve your dreams, but later

So, if you can accept everything and work towards coming out of the pit, you can also learn to accept everything and work towards getting rid of your ROCD. For example, if you wear glasses, you do not lose sleep over it, and do not hold it against yourself that you wear glasses. (At least I hope you don't). You acknowledge that your vision is not perfect without glasses and you accept the need to wear glasses.

Similarly, when a girl menstruates, she may experience three to five days of discomfort, pain, irritation, cramps, and so on. Yet, girls learn to accept it as a part of their life and do not deny its existence. These are examples learning to accept unpleasantness in our lives. Similarly, ROCD is an unpleasant disorder. But the more we learn to accept it, the better we are at dealing with it. Thus acceptance is very important to the recovery process in ROCD.

There is a self-administered psychometric test called the Acceptance and Action Questionnaire-Revised (AAQ-2; Bond et al., 2011) that has been provided as PT4 in the Worksheets file. The AAQ-2 tests your psychological flexibility, that is, how accepting you are of your situations and how you act when life throws a curve ball at you. Take the test and make a note of your psychological flexibility. Remember that the higher you score, the more inflexible you are. You will need to work towards lowering your score to be more accepting of your situation. We shall be exploring this in detail later when we get to the recovery section.

In the next chapter, we shall understand the problem some people have with acceptance.

To-Do:
Complete PT4 - AAQ-2

S2C13. The problem with acceptance

When I talk to people and mention acceptance to them, sometimes the skepticism is so palpable, I can almost touch it. The apprehension is *'What if my acceptance of my thoughts leads to its manifestation due to the law of attraction as laid out in Rhonda Byrne's book, The Secret? What if I actually cause my thoughts to come real by accepting them?'* You may feel that even the thought of committing an action increases the possibility of committing it, a belief observed in people with OCD (Butchler et al., 2013). I am going to try and address that 'what if' in this chapter.

First and foremost, this thought itself is a Meta OCD thought. It starts with a 'what-if' and it causes anxiety. If you try to accept your ROCD thoughts, this worry about the law of attraction becomes dominant and sticky. You may feel an urgent need to do something about it and dispel it. Hence, it is a Meta OCD thought and needs to be handled like any other obsessive thought.

Second, the law of attraction propounds that we attract only when we desire and expect the same thing together. When the desire and expectation do not match, the law of attraction does not come true. In the context of your ROCD, your desire may be to accept the thoughts but you may expecting them to come true (and hence the fear). So, if the law of attraction has to truly work, your thoughts in ROCD cannot come true because of the difference between your desire (to get better) and your expectation (that you won't get better).

Third, consider this example. Let us say you want to attract career success. When you say you are expecting to succeed and you desire to succeed, everything you do, becomes goal directed. If you want to succeed but your efforts are missing, you do not desire to succeed enough. On the other hand, if you keep putting in efforts recklessly, you probably do not expect to succeed and hence keep the excessive effort.

Since one of the elements is missing, success becomes elusive. However, if you put both of them in the right measure, success is inevitable. So, the law of attraction is not magic. It is goal directed effort. You will not attract a million dollars out of nowhere. Similarly, you will not attract your obsessions to come true simply if you accept them. On the contrary, you will attract recovery if you desire to recover and expect to recover through acceptance. With this understanding, the law of attraction can be actively used to aid in the recovery process through complete acceptance.

One of the common questions on acceptance is - *does that mean I should accept an abusive relationship?* The answer is a loud no. Of course, abusive relationships are not to be accepted. What is to be accepted is the psychological aspect of it, that is, your response to it. If you are in an abusive relationship and you sulk, cry, and lament that your relationship is bad, you are accepting the abusive relationship, not the psychological aspect of it. If you do not accept the abusive relationship, but understand that if you continue to keep it unchecked, the abuse will continue, you accept the psychological aspect. Then, you feel more empowered to change the equation by standing up for yourself or ending the abusive relationship. Hence, when we refer to acceptance, we refer to accepting the effect the problem has on us and changing what we can to make it better.

In the next chapter, we shall discuss the concept of gratitude, which is the fifth pillar.

S2C14. The fifth pillar - Gratitude

When you are struggling, it is difficult to find things to be grateful for. *'What part of my life you think is worth being thankful for?'* you may ask. Your pain may blindside you to the things that you could possibly be grateful for. Even if you could see them, (which most times you can) you would not be inclined to look at them with any feelings of appreciation. Here is where I want to point out one fundamental difference between what the attitude of gratitude is commonly understood as, and what it actually is.

The attitude of gratitude is commonly understood as being thankful for what you have and others don't. That is to an extent correct, but not enough or palatable. For example, if you're going through a tough time with your ROCD, and if you're told *'Look at kids in Somalia, they don't even have food'*, you'll probably dismiss this line of reasoning, because how does their not having food reduce the amount of suffering you're going through? Trying to tell you that someone else is suffering more may seem like trivializing your pain - as if to say your suffering isn't bad enough and hence not important enough.

Thus, while the attitude of gratitude does mean being thankful to the universe for what you have and for the positive in the world (Jans-Beken et al., 2020), this definition in my opinion, doesn't cover it all. The attitude of gratitude is the recognition of how much more you have over what you *think* you have. This definition doesn't look at anyone else's lot, but only at yours. Stop, look, listen - you may have a hundred more things to be thankful for than you realize. Those hundred things may still not provide a life that you'd be totally happy with, I agree. But those hundred things have already made your life better than you think it is.

So, in order to be truly grateful, you don't have to only think of things that make you proverbially jump with joy. Like, you don't have to win a lottery or you don't have to get a promotion, or your ROCD does not have to disappear. Understandably, if those are things that you're looking for, you'll find very few of them. Instead, look for things that would make your life worse if you didn't have them. For example, if you like coffee and you're getting your cup of coffee every morning, be grateful. What if it were to suddenly become unavailable? Would it not matter? Would it not make your life a tad worse? Why not appreciate it then?

How about running water? The ability to take a shower whenever you want? A bed to sleep in, however hard? A job, however unsatisfying? To reiterate, the point isn't about how much joy they add to your life right now. The point is how much misery or at least discomfort they'd add to your life if they were to be taken away. Or, alternatively, think about what you do not have in your life that would make your life miserable if you had to deal with it. Like toxic parents, for example. Or a physical handicap. If you don't have these, aren't you better off than you think you are? Think about that. And be grateful.

But what does it have to do with ROCD? A lot. The Greater Good Science Center at UC Berkeley conducted a study in 2017 and found that people seeking mental health counseling and practicing gratitude showed significantly improved mental health, with lowered depression and anxiety. When you practice gratitude, you can reap some benefits. Make it a habit over a period of time to look for things for which you can be grateful. You do not have to ignore what is not working in your life. You do have to be aware of those aspects to be able to work on changing them. But you also do not lose sight of what you have and thank your stars, your God, the powers that be, or whoever you want to be thankful to, for them.

I have included a link to an article on Gratitude at the end of this chapter. Be sure to access it and read it. Also, get into the practice of filling in the gratitude journal every day. Each day find three simple things to be grateful about and fill in the Gratitude Worksheet in Worksheet 9 (available at the end of this course book and also in the Worksheets file) to become more aware of what you have in your life that you have been ignoring, that you can be thankful for. Both your partner and you can develop this practice to see your overall outlook change. Try to focus on gratitude towards your partner and for all the support you have been receiving in your journey.

In the next chapter, we shall look at the next pillar of recovery that is insight.

To-Do:
Read the gratitude article from https://t.ly/lcD_
Fill WS9 - the gratitude journal

S2C15. The sixth pillar - Insight

Psychological insight simply put means awareness of the rationality or irrationality of one's thoughts. Insight is important in the maintenance of and recovery from several mental disorders. Lack of insight can signify how long the recovery process can take. As an analogy, consider an alcoholic who goes to a counselor to give up drinking. If he has the insight that he has a drinking problem, he is more likely to put in more effort at tolerating the discomfort that comes with not drinking. However, if the person does not have sufficient insight, the person may not believe he has a problem and may only work on things that are easy in the recovery process. The moment something gets difficult, the person may give up either citing it as too difficult or unnecessary. In this example, low insight may lead to lesser effort which may steamroll recovery, whereas high insight may lead to better effort, and may aid the recovery process.

A person with ROCD knows that his thoughts are irrational. But when he is triggered the thoughts seem so real that he begins to believe in them and does compulsions to make the thoughts go away. If he begins to believe that his thoughts are not irrational, he can be said to have low insight. He may think that others are wrong. He may consider needing to get his girlfriend's text all the time to know where she is as a rational requirement, in the name of love. But, that may be an erroneous belief. Depending on their insight, sufferers decide whether their behavior is rational or irrational (Abramowitz & Jacoby, 2015). Depending upon the insight, the speed of recovery may also vary.

In the Worksheets file, PT5 is the Brown's Assessment of Beliefs Scale (BABS; Eisen et al., 1998). Complete it to know your levels of insight. Low scores indicate low insight. This score needs to be raised through cognitive restructuring for improving insight.

In the next chapter, we shall explore the seventh pillar of recovery, which is compassion.

To-Do:
Complete PT5 - BABS

S2C16. The seventh pillar - Compassion

The seventh pillar of recovery is compassion. Compassion has been defined as a feeling "that arises in witnessing another's suffering and that motivates a subsequent desire to help" (Goetz et al., 2010, p. 351). It means being aware of another person's suffering and wanting to take steps to reduce it. Compassion refers to understanding, love and acceptance of others. Compassion is showing empathy towards people who are struggling. Self-compassion refers to experiencing these feelings for self.

Compassion is critical both towards the world and towards self. In the context of ROCD, compassion towards both yourself and your partner is critical to recovery. Neither does compassion towards your partner make you weak, nor does self-compassion make you indulgent and selfish.

When you are triggered you may feel that your partner is imperfect and that you are making a mistake by continuing to be in the relationship. However, your true feelings for her may not allow you to break up and this conflict may cause distress. This may result in you trying to either change your partner or getting into arguments with her and being hurtful to her.

If your partner understands that your ROCD is making you hurtful, she may continue to support you despite being upset. She therefore deserves your compassion, love, understanding and empathy from you for tolerating your barbs.

At the same time, you also deserve self-compassion for struggling to make sense of your thoughts and feelings. If your struggles make you feel ashamed of yourself because of what you put your partner through, you need to stop judging yourself poorly and show yourself some love, while managing your behavior towards your partner.

Similarly when you are triggered you may feel that your partner does not love you enough and you may long for her to show you affection in a manner that will satisfy you. You may understand in moments of clarity that your expectations may be unreasonable and your conclusions may be faulty, but the distress may seem real and incapacitating. At that moment, you need to engage in self-compassion for going through the struggle.

Similarly, you need to practice compassion towards all the people in your life who help you manage your ROCD. This could be your parents, your friends, your siblings, or your co-workers. If they do not understand your struggle, but still try to be there for you, they deserve your compassion.

In the Worksheets file, there is another psychometric test provided called the Self-Compassion Scale (Neff, 2003) in PT6. Take the test and note your self-compassion levels. The ready reckoner sheet will show you the dimensions of self-compassion and where you stand on each of them. Being more aware of your levels of self-compassion will be the first step towards making changes to improve the levels and help you recover faster.

In the next chapter, we shall look at the next four pillars of recovery viz., diet, sleep, exercise and supplements.

To-Do:
Complete PT6 - SCS

S2C17. The next four pillars

In this chapter, I shall briefly touch upon the next four pillars of recovery. After CBT, ERP, mindfulness, acceptance, gratitude, insight and compassion, the eighth pillar is a good diet. There is evidence that shows that certain types of foods can cause anxiety and certain types of foods can relieve anxiety. Foods high in tryptophan can boost the production of serotonin in the brain (Strasser et al., 2016), apart from offering other benefits. Foods high in tryptophan are whole milk, fish, turkey, chicken, oats, cheese, nuts, seeds, whole grain bread, chocolate, fruits, leafy vegetables like spinach, etc. Good quality animal protein, good quality fats, vegetables, fruits, water, probiotics like sauerkraut or yogurt, nuts (pre-soaked in water to remove the anti-nutrients), lentils (pre-soaked to remove the phytates) are all good for the gut and mental health.

On the flip side, foods containing sugar, alcohol, caffeine, processed flour, aspartame (which is an artificial sweetener), are likely to cause a spike in anxiety or depressive symptoms (Robinson, 2021) and should be either entirely eliminated from the diet or at least, consumed in moderation. Vegetable oils are not as healthy as they claim to be. Simple carbohydrates convert to sugar, so they should be consumed in moderation. Sodas, colas and energy drinks should be avoided. Gluten should be minimized as it may result in a leaky gut and affect mental wellbeing. Smoking is a no-no, even though it may seem to you sometimes that smoking relieves anxiety (which you know is not true). Hence, a good diet is the eighth pillar of recovery.

The ninth pillar of recovery is sleep. Good sleep is very important for mental well being. Sleep and mental health have a two-way relationship. While poor mental health can cause sleep problems, poor sleep can worsen mental health issues as well (Dahl, & Harvey, 2007). When you don't sleep well, you automatically become more susceptible to stress, depression and anxiety. Sleep would help you recover from physical and mental exertion and if sleep is inadequate, recovery is inadequate. Hence, good sleep is the ninth pillar of recovery. At the end of this course book, I have included an article on how to sleep better as Additional Resource 3. Do read that as well.

The tenth pillar of recovery is physical exercise. Exercise is important to make sure that your mental well being is maintained (Ratey, 2019). Exercise has many benefits. It can help you sleep better, which is good for mental health. Exercise can boost happy hormones such as serotonin, relaxation hormones such as GABA, which serve to lift your mood and relieve stress and anxiety and endorphins which enable you to focus better and improve mindfulness. Exercise boosts neural growth, which helps to break old habits and form new ones. Exercise also makes you more resilient and can make you feel ready for everything that life throws at you. For these reasons, exercise is the tenth pillar of recovery.

The eleventh pillar of recovery is supplements. Dietary supplements, that is. It is well known that the absence of vitamins and minerals in the body may lead to physical problems. It is relatively lesser known that this absence may hamper mental health as well. There is evidence that taking dietary supplements can help mental health (Hoffman et al., 2019). For example, deficiency of vitamin B could impact cognitive function and memory. Deficiency of folic acid (vitamin B9) can cause depressive symptoms. Deficiency of thiamin (vitamin B1) may cause anxiety. Dietary supplements to augment these depleted vitamins can help resolve the associated issues. Supplements containing vitamin B12, vitamin D, Omega-3 fatty acids, zinc, magnesium, and creatine can also boost mental health. Supplements, thus, are the eleventh pillar of recovery. Hence, exercise, good sleep, good diet and dietary supplements are important pillars to recovery.

In the next chapter, we shall look at the twelfth pillar of recovery that is medicine.

To-Do:
Read AR3 - 23 tips to sleep better

S2C18. The twelfth pillar - Medicines

The twelfth pillar of recovery is medicines. One section of people is averse to taking medicines because of the various side-effects. Plus, medicines do not *cure* OCD, they only *treat* OCD. So, there is a large chunk of people which does not want to take medicines. The anti-medicine community may quote a lot of research which shows how psychiatric medicines impact a person's physical health, how medicines are not as effective as therapy, and how there are significant side effects. All of that is partly true. But mental issues do not always have just a psychological component. They have a biological component as well. So, realigning what is out of alignment may sometimes require medication.

Being dismissive of medicines because they have side effects amounts to choosing ROCD over a few (and mostly temporary) side effects. It is like the poem 'The Blind Men and the Elephant' by John Godfrey Saxe. The six blind men go to observe an elephant and then describe it. Since each person is only focusing on one part, each describes the elephant differently.

One touches the tail and says the elephant is like a rope. Another touches the trunk and says that the elephant is like a snake. The third person touches a leg and says that the elephant is like a tree. The fourth person touches the ear and says that the elephant is like a fan. The fifth touches the sharp tusk and says that the elephant is like a spear. The sixth one touches the body of the elephant and says that it is like a wall. All of them were partly right, but they did not see the complete picture. I have added the poem at the end of this course book as Additional Resource 4. Take a break, read the poem, and enjoy it.

Medicines are like that. True there are side effects, some worse than others. But most of the side effects abate. If they don't, doctors can calibrate the dosage or the medicines to lessen them. If they still don't, it is the choice you make - whether the side effects are worse than ROCD. Medicines may also take up to six weeks to start showing effect. Most people tend to give up taking medicines if they don't seem to work in a week or ten days.

The other refrain is that medicines are habit forming. Again, this is an overgeneralization. The three most common types of medicines prescri-

-bed for OCD are SSRIs, benzodiazepines and anti-psychotics. SSRIs make sure that the serotonin produced in the brain and gut is available to the brain before it completes its function and gets reabsorbed. Dr. David Burns uses a wonderful analogy in his book 'Feeling Good'. Think of it like needing to cross a lake over to the other side but not being able to because you don't have a boat. So, an SSRI enables the serotonin molecules to be available as boats to transmit messages across neural pathways in the brain. SSRIs may cause some withdrawal symptoms with discontinuation but are not habit-forming (Fava et al., 2015).

The second type of medicine that is prescribed, often to relieve anxiety is a benzodiazepine. Benzodiazepines are believed to be habit forming, since they provide immediate relief and hence there is a possibility of abuse (Evans & Sullivan, 2014). Hence benzodiazepines are prescribed for a short duration only, or on an SOS basis.

The third type of medicine that may be prescribed sometimes is a mild anti-psychotic, to augment the efficacy of SSRIs and improve psychological insight, which is sometimes missing. Even SSRIs work to improve insight. But in some cases, an anti-psychotic may be added too. Anti-psychotics are also associated with symptoms of discontinuation (Brandt et al., 2020) but are not habit-forming either.

Sometimes, doctors may prescribe SNRIs or other anti-depressants. Or in the case of some co-morbidity, some other class of drugs. But whatever the doctors prescribe, you should put complete faith in and be compliant with the medication. Non-compliance is one of the major problems where medication for psychiatric disorders is concerned. If recovery is the core objective, medicines may be necessary sometimes.

This completes the twelve pillars of recovery and also concludes this section. In the next section, we shall get down to understanding concepts you need to understand to get better.

To-Do:
Read AR4 - 'The Blind Men and the Elephant' for fun

Section III: Concepts You Should Know

S3C1. Naming your ROCD

Sometimes it helps to give your ROCD a name (Prudovski, n.d.). That is, think of your ROCD as a separate person. You probably already think of your ROCD as another person because it seems to wield power over you and make you do things you know you should not. You seem to operate on the orders of another person.

Hmm, so let's look at it again. This person has power over you. This person makes you do things that you don't want to do. If you don't do its bidding, you feel anxious. What kind of a person would do that? A benevolent person who has your best interests in mind? Or a toxic person who is selfish and is thinking only of himself regardless of the emotional cost to you? I am sure you would agree that it is the latter. A toxic person who is definitely not a friend, but perhaps an irritant or a fear in your life. Once again, do realize that ROCD is not your friend but someone you don't want in your life.

So think back on your life. Think of a person you dislike, fear, or have been traumatized by. You may have had a toxic boss or a toxic family member. You may have had a friend who betrayed your trust and you couldn't trust him anymore. Or it may be a person who you know is interested in your partner and will do anything to cause you to breakup with your partner and be with her instead. Think about this toxic person and think of his name. You may be inwardly cringing or may be feeling anxious. You know that if he asked you to do anything, it would have a selfish motive. You know that if he gave you any advice, it would definitely be the wrong advice. You know that following whatever that person says to you is a recipe for doom. So, if the advice is coming from him, you would dismiss it even if the advice feels like the right thing to do.

It may help to call your ROCD by that name. Knowing that that person is bad news for you in your life, believe that the person has not changed and will continue to hurt you at every possible opportunity. Therefore, everything said to you by your ROCD is to be looked at with the same mistrust and disbelief.

Let us say that in school you had a friend by the name of Kay who had betrayed your trust. Kay pretended to be your friend but called you names and laughed at you behind your back. When you found out and confronted Kay, you realized that Kay was never your friend, but was always in the *other camp*, so to speak. You stopped being friends with Kay and decided that you could never trust Kay again.

Start by calling your ROCD Kay. Believe that whatever your ROCD says to you is coming from Kay, something that cannot be trusted. So, when there is an obsessive thought in your head, mindfully remind yourself that despite this seeming real, it is Kay who is doing this to you. Kay is advising you to believe that you do not love your partner. Kay is advising you to compare and find flaws. Kay is advising you to criticize your partner. Kay just wants to create a rift between you and your partner.

This means that nothing your ROCD says can be trusted. When you arrive at that conclusion, every time you have an urge to do a compulsion, if you recognize it mindfully, resist the urge. You may be able to resist the temptation to do your compulsions if you believe that Kay is urging you to do them and Kay does not have your best interests in mind.

If you did not have ROCD and if Kay told you to criticize your partner for a flaw, you wouldn't do that. In the same way, if you get the urge to criticize your partner for a flaw, resist it by recognizing that Kay is asking you to do it, so that you have a fall out with your partner.

Again, if you did not have ROCD and your partner did not text you immediately after you sent her a text, or if the text from your partner is not how you expected it to be, you would not fight with your partner on Kay's say so. So, if you get the urge to call up your partner and scream at her for not replying to your text immediately or for not having texted as per your exact expectations, resist the temptation to do so. Understand that Kay is again making you do that so that the rift between you and your partner increases.

Remember this name as this name will be important in your recovery process. If you do not have any specific person in mind for the purpose, you can give your ROCD the name of a negative character from a book or a movie or call it Satan or Devil. For the purpose of this course book, we shall continue to interchangeably refer to your ROCD as ROCD or Kay.

In the next chapter, we will understand another important concept of triggered and non-triggered states.

S3C2. Triggered vs non-triggered states

In this chapter, I am going to explain the critical distinction between the two states of being triggered and not being triggered. Sometimes people say distraction is important, and at other times they say distraction is a compulsion. Sometimes people talk about rationalizing the irrational thought and at other times call it a compulsion. Sometimes people stress on the importance of seeking clarification, while at other times call it a compulsion. So, what is it really? Are these things important or are these compulsions?

Welcome to the complexity of OCD, because they are both. They can be either, depending upon how they are used - or more importantly, when they are used. This brings us to the two states of mind - triggered versus non-triggered. Some of these actions can be done when triggered, others when not triggered. I shall explain how this works with an analogy first and then with specific reference to ROCD.

Think of having to write an exam. When you are sitting in the examination hall, which is likened to the triggered state, access to text books and reading material is disallowed. You are not allowed to access Google to search for your answers, or refer to notes or confirm with your friends if your answers are correct. But when you are preparing for the exam or after you are done with it, (the non-triggered state) all of these activities are not only allowed, but also highly recommended; so that you remember the stuff you are going to be tested on. Thus, you can refer to all course material before and after the exam.

Hence, in the case of your ROCD, all the rationalization and clarification that you would like to do is allowed only outside the triggered state. Doing any of these activities when you are triggered is the compulsion. For example you may see a pretty girl and begin to think that your partner is not as pretty as this girl, making you wonder if you are in the right relationship. That is the triggered state.

In this state, as mentioned, there can be no rationalization. There can be no comparison for the sake of clarity. There can be no reassurance seeking for the sake of clarity. Doing any of this is similar to cheating in the exam. This is not allowed. If you do these when you are triggered, they become compulsions. At this point you are expected to power through with the resistance to compulsion without rationalizing the need to not do it. But when you are not triggered, that is when you understand the irrationality of your thoughts your therapist will engage you in cognitive therapy and rationalize these fears for you. Then, it is a technique to help you get better.

However, there is another important consideration. ROCD is not as distinct and compartmentalized as being inside or outside an examination hall. The state of non-trigger may easily segue into the state of trigger. If the rationalization process is on during the transition, something that started off as a technique could easily become a compulsion.

Hence, utmost care is needed to ensure that the rationalization is being done only when you are not triggered at all. I will keep emphasizing on this at various points throughout the course book so that you internalize it well and do not make mistakes. This distinction between triggered and non-triggered states is a critical distinction and needs to be understood well for recovery.

The MMA super vision will help you understand this distinction better. Make sure to have a clear demarcation between the two states, even though they seem to blend into one another most times.

In the next chapter we shall talk about the MMA super vision.

S3C3. The MMA super vision

When ROCD first hits, we do the compulsions because they seem like the right thing to do to help us out of our misery. But even when we get to know that the compulsions don't help us but hold us back, we still continue to do them. At times, we do not even realize that we are engaging in compulsions. At other times, even though we realize it, we are unable to stop them. Why? Why is it so difficult to stop the compulsions? What can we do to stop these compulsions? The solution to some extent lies in the development of the mindfulness-mindfulness-acceptance (MMA) super vision. I shall try to explain what the MMA super vision is with the help of a few figures.

Figure 3.3.1: The trigger zone

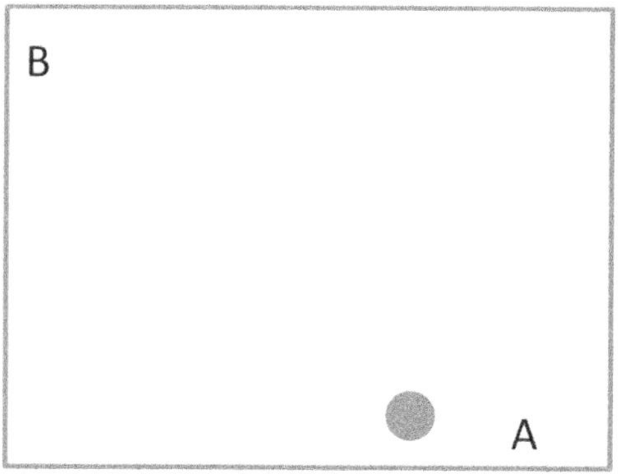

Refer to figure 3.3.1. You are the grey dot that needs to travel from A to B. The entire area is a trigger zone for you. Figure 3.3.1 may represent spending time with your partner and travelling from A to B may represent watching a romantic movie with her. You can't see it very clearly but there is a faint border that you should not cross over because on the other side are some obstacles. The border represents the border between your non-triggered and triggered states and the obstacles are your compulsions.

As you keep travelling from A to B, since the border is not very visible, you end up crossing the border as shown in figure 3.3.2. Thus, you get into the triggered zone without consciously realizing it. Since you are not conscious of the crossing over, you engage in your compulsions even

Figure 3.3.2: Crossing over to the triggered state

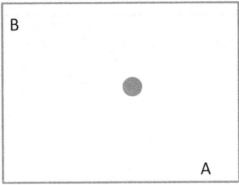

before you know it. Only after the trigger has subsided do you realize that once again your ROCD has won.

Enter mindfulness. Through the practice of mindfulness, you begin to identify your trigger zones even *before* you enter the trigger zone. As shown in figure 3.3.3, the light bulb on the bottom-left is your mindfulness (the first M of the MMA super vision) before you enter the trigger zone. Thus, when you spend time with your partner and think of watching a romantic movie with her, you realize mindfully that you are likely to get triggered. In diagram 3.3.3 as you can see, the border between the non-triggered and triggered states has become more visible.

Figure 3.3.3: The first mindfulness point

Figure 3.3.4: The visible border

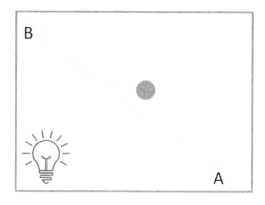

However, even though you are mindful at this stage, if you cross over to the triggered state (as you often will) and become unmindful once again, you will not notice when you end up doing your compulsions. As you can see in figure 3.3.4, you are in the triggered zone but the compulsions are not visible to you and you may end up running into them.

At this stage, if you again bring yourself to become mindful (the second M of the MMA super vision), and recognize that you are in the triggered zone, you become more aware of the obstacles in your way, i.e., your compulsions. In figure 3.3.5, the bulb on the top-right is the second M in the MMA super vision. As you can see, the line between the non-triggered and triggered state is also clearer and well-formed and the obstacles (the triangles) are also visible.

Figure 3.3.5: The second mindfulness point

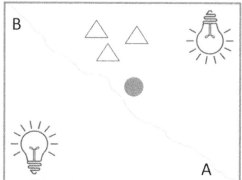

However, even at this stage, your ROCD may tell you '*Why bother trying to resist? Just do your compulsions and be done with it*'. At this stage, your acceptance (the A of the MMA super vision) of your ROCD, of the compulsions it asks you to do, and of the importance of not doing those compulsions will complete the super vision.

Figure 3.3.6: The point of acceptance

If you accept that you do not need to do the compulsions to survive the trigger zone, you can cross over to B without needing to do your compulsions, as shown in figure 3.3.6. You become stronger and your compulsions become weaker and disperse as you power through.

When you do not recognize that you could move into the triggered state, you may end up moving into the triggered zone and doing the compulsions out of unmindfulness. Even if you are mindful before you enter the triggered zone, you could become unmindful after you enter it and may end up doing your compulsions. Only when you are mindful before and after entering the triggered zone and accept that you do not need to do the compulsions to survive, that is, only when you use your MMA super vision, do you achieve mastery over your ROCD.

In the next chapter we shall look at the stages of compulsion handling.

S3C4. The stages of compulsion handling

When you first start obsessing about your relationship, you don't immediately recognize your ROCD like you would recognize a headache. By the time you do and discover you have ROCD, a lot of time is likely to have elapsed. In that time, you might end up developing many compulsive rituals, both physical and mental. Some of them may have become so internalized that you may not even look upon them as compulsive rituals but just as quirks.

This leads to many rituals remaining unnoticed and under the radar. When you seek treatment, you may not mention these rituals because you may not be aware of them yourself. For example, you may have stopped meeting one particular friend socially because you may think her relationship is better than yours and you don't want to be triggered. You may not consider this as an important point to mention during therapy. However, it is an important aspect which keeps your ROCD strong and hence needs resolution.

Additionally, whatever rituals you develop are likely to have core fears that need to be identified as well. Most times, you may not even realize that there are core fears getting you to do the rituals. For example, you may fear an abusive relationship in future similar to a news article you read and hence may want to make sure your partner is perfect. Your fear of the abuse and the pain may be stronger than getting into the wrong relationship. You may not even mention the fear of pain during therapy but it needs resolution for you to feel better.

So, when you start the recovery process, there are three stages that you might have to go through with each compulsion before you learn to handle them.

Awareness: In this stage, you begin to gain knowledge about and understand all your compulsive rituals. Avoidance of meeting people who remind you of your fears is a compulsion. If this is not identified, it may remain unresolved. In the second example, you are explained that the fear of pain and abuse needs resolution too and not just the fear of being in the wrong relationship. If you don't understand the core fear, you may keep working on the fear of being in the wrong relationship and struggle to deal with it when it doesn't seem to seem to make you feel better. The fear of the pain and abuse may appear through some other compulsive ritual and the cycle may keep repeating. Knowledge and understanding will help you identify what and how much needs to be dealt with. Along with it, the knowledge of how to handle the obsessions is also important.

Recall: Awareness is not always sufficient, particularly in ROCD. Even with the knowledge and understanding of what needs to be handled and how, you may not be able to. When it is time to face the fear, that is when you are triggered, the obsession may be bad and the thought may seem real. You may not be able to remember what you know and have understood. So, you may not remember that avoiding social contact is incorrect, and that you need to risk the pain if you are to get over your ROCD. But with repeated reminders and with the strengthening of your mindfulness muscle, you may finally begin to remember. Thus, the second stage in recovery is remembering the knowledge gained in the triggered state.

Action: When you gain knowledge and understanding, and begin to remember that the rituals are not to be performed when you are triggered, the third stage, which is action, becomes possible. In this stage you decide to either perform your rituals or stay away from them. Even though you may have gained knowledge and understanding, and even though you may remember what you are supposed to do, taking action to stop ritualistic behavior is not going to be easy. But with repeated reminders and with better acceptance of the need to not do the compulsions, you may begin to take action.

When you are triggered and want to cancel a social engagement with that friend, you may remember that it is unhelpful and despite what your ROCD asks you to do you choose to meet the friend. Similarly, when you wonder if your relationship is right, you may remember that you are supposed to risk future pain and continue to be anchored in the relationship right now, despite the fear. When you continue to do the difficult things, you are taking action.

Thus, in the beginning, you may not even be aware of where you are going wrong. With knowledge and understanding you become more aware. When you are triggered, with sufficient effort and mindfulness you may begin to remember more often not to act upon your compulsive urges. With practice and acceptance of the futility of doing the compulsions, you may begin to take action to resist the urges.

In the beginning, maybe out of the ten times you are likely to get triggered, you may recognize the pre-trigger signs only once. Out of the ten times you are triggered and get the urge to do your compulsions, you may mindfully remember only once to not do your compulsions. And out of the ten times you remember not to act upon your urges compulsively, you may accept the situation and succeed in not doing your compulsions only once. But slowly, with repeated practice, and with your MMA super vision getting stronger, the number of times you recognize, remember and resist the urges will increase and you will begin to inch your way towards recovery.

In the next chapter, we shall understand the difference between plain response prevention and ERP.

S3C5. Response prevention vs ERP

Sometimes the ROCD may impair the major part of the day and you may begin to say *'I am always triggered'*. But that is not entirely true. There are moments of clarity which help you understand the irrationality of your triggers. Those are the moments when you feel that you don't want to let go of your partner, regardless of what your OCD tells you. They may be few and far between but they are there for sure. That is the reason why you are reading this course book.

Getting exposed to a trigger without you being prepared for it is not a deliberate exposure. It is accidental exposure. Imagine you are sitting on a beach with your back to the waves and a wave slams into you from behind. You will probably get a shock and will be more flustered if you are not ready for the wave. That is accidental exposure.

But if you sit facing the waves, you can see when the wave is about to hit you. If you let it hit you, you are still going to be shocked but lesser so (you are going to be able to brace yourself for the impact). That is deliberate exposure. Hence, deliberate exposures are a key requirement to being able to manage the process of recovery better.

Thus, response prevention (RP) is trying to not do a compulsion when you have accidental or unavoidable exposures. ERP is when you deliberately expose yourself to your triggers and learn to manage them without compulsive behavior. ERP is better than just response prevention because one, you can decide on the time when you would like to face your fears and hence be prepared for them. Two, you can decide on the intensity of exposures and choose not to overwhelm yourself with anxiety

Three, before engaging in ERP, you would observe your behavior and list down your compulsions, even those that have been normalized in your life. When you observe your behavior, you begin to see how many more things have come under the fold of ROCD without your conscious realization. ERP would help in dealing with all these concerns. Hence for these reasons, ERP is more effective than just RP.

In the next chapter we shall understand the concept of neuroplasticity.

S3C6. Neuroplasticity

When we get into the rationalization of all compulsions, you will observe that the methodology for dealing with all of them is almost the same. Why, you would ask. If you observe how your ROCD works on you systematically and repeatedly, you realize that repetition of your obsessive thoughts and compulsive behaviors is largely instrumental in strengthening your ROCD. You have the same thought, you learn through trial and error to perform a specific physical or mental compulsion, and keep providing the same compulsive response every time you have the thought. After a point, the compulsive response to the thought goes on auto-pilot. This leads to the compulsive response becoming a habit that is difficult to break.

Hence, when we respond to the compulsion, we need to pay our ROCD back in the same coin - through repetition. Repeating the response prevention script, both in the triggered and non-triggered states repeatedly will enable better internalization. Sort of like the multiplication tables that you learn through repetition. You read and re-read and memorize the multiplication tables when you can, so that you are able to remember them when you need them. Similarly, when you read and re-read the response prevention script repeatedly, you may be able to access it when you need it, irrespective of the compulsion your ROCD forces you to do. For that, we have to train and rewire the brain.

Our brain has an amazing property called neuroplasticity. Simply put, neuroplasticity is the ability of the brain to break old habits and form new ones. No matter what our age, we can always learn new skills and forget old habits that do not serve us. However, the brain needs to be rewired to form new habits, which takes time. If you want to learn football, you must constantly go to the field and practice. The more you practice, the better you will get at it. Or even if you want to learn cooking, you cannot become an expert at it in one day.

Depending upon what we have been doing all our lives, which actions we have been repeating, which actions we have stayed away from, our brain gets wired. The things we do often, become easy for us. We do not have to think about them, while doing them. This includes both good habits and bad. Like, brushing our teeth. We do it every morning and evening. We have been doing it for years, so we know how to do it. We don't have to think about it. But some of our activities may be relatively new and we may not have gotten into the habit of doing them yet. That is to say, our brains have not yet been wired for those activities yet.

Figure 3.6.1: A well-trodden path

Consider figure 3.6.1. It is of a well trodden path. Before this path existed, there may have been shrubbery growing here. But with constant use, a path began to get formed and it became bereft of the shrubs. It is easier to walk this path for people than form a new one.

Now, assume that you want to create a new path three feet to the left or right of this path and stop using this path. Can it be done? Yes, it can be done. But people will have to stop using this path and start walking on the shrubs where they want the new path to be. Will it get made in a day? Two days? No. It will take a while. But with regular usage only. It won't do for people to give up midway and walk the old path. If that happens, neither will the new path be formed, nor will the old path be unformed. But if there is persistence, bit by bit, a new path will begin to emerge and the old path, due to disuse will start disappearing. Slowly. But after some time, one will not even know if the old path ever existed.

Rewiring the brain is like that. It involves breaking old patterns and forming new ones. The old path represents the habit you're trying to break. The new path is the new habit. It is possible but it is not easy. But it can be done. 100 percent of the times, if the effort is put in. Stick to a new habit, despite it being difficult and despite the temptation of falling into the old one, and with sufficient practice, the old bad habit will have been eliminated and the new good habit will have been adopted. And that is when you would have succeeded in rewiring the brain.

Hence, the repetitive nature of the ROCD script will help in faster rewiring of the brain. The sooner you internalize the healthier response, the more adept you will become at offering it and dealing with your compulsions better. This is the rationale of the repetitiveness of the response prevention script.

In the next chapter we shall look at what progress in ERP means.

S3C7. Progress in ERP

There seems to be a common misconception among people that they would be expected to stop everything all at once. Some people come for therapy with a feeling of hopelessness and claim that they have tried to stop their compulsions themselves but have not succeeded. But progress in ERP does not mean elimination of bad thoughts. It means a systematic reduction in compulsions, through a process of learning.

Think of a small child who goes into the first grade. If he is shown a book of advanced mathematics, he is going to panic. He may begin to believe that he cannot handle it, and he would be right. He would not be able to handle such advanced concepts. But he is not even expected to handle that at his age. He is expected to understand basic addition. As he grows, he would be taught to handle more complex concepts and then eventually he may graduate to advanced concepts.

In a similar way, when you start doing ERP, you are in the first grade, metaphorically speaking. You need to only handle those obsessions and resist those compulsions that are the easiest. The time for handling bigger ones will come later. If you try to handle everything together, you will fail. Not *you may*. *You will*. If you don't even try because you think that it will be too much, you may be giving up because you expect the first grader in you to be able to handle advanced mathematics. This is bound to seem like an impossible task.

So, first things first, you need to truly understand that the recovery process will be slow and will need lots of practice in strengthening fundamentals. Progress in ROCD can be measured in a number of different ways that I want to talk about.

- Compulsions may be reduced in duration. If you are engaged in episodes of rumination, and your typical rumination episode lasts for one hour, reducing that to fifty minutes is progress.
- Compulsions may be reduced in frequency. If you are engaged in a compulsion of checking Instagram posts to see whether you like the way your partner looks or not and your checking involves going through fifty pictures at a time, progress would mean bringing this down to forty-five pictures.

- Compulsions may be reduced by creating a gap between the obsession and compulsion or between two instances of compulsions. If you are engaged in the compulsion of reassurance seeking from your partner or some friend about the rightness of your relationship, you may wait for ten minutes between the trigger and the reassurance seeking, or between two instances of reassurance seeking. Doing even so much, is progress.

Often, sadly small progress is dismissed as zero-progress. People may think that you are not putting in enough effort. This may deter you because you know how much effort you are putting in to bring about small changes. You may need to learn to pat yourself on the back for the effort made. And you may need to build on the success you have experienced, no matter how small.

Another concern people have is that it would take a very long time to recover if progress is so slow. Well, yes. It may, and it probably will. But, the alternative is to continue to struggle for life. Besides, as you get better at managing your compulsions, progress is much faster. You will be able to handle more as you progress in your recovery journey. So, while all this may seem overwhelming and never ending when you start, it really won't be. You need to just push your way through the first few weeks or months of excruciating work before it starts seeming simple and doable.

Yet another expectation from ERP people with ROCD may have is gaining certainty in their relationships. But even people who do not have ROCD can never be (or remain) certain about their relationships. So, ERP will not result in the perfect relationship. It can make you look at your imperfect relationship (with your partner's imperfections and also your own) more adaptively, though, so that you can live a happy life. That is the simple goal that you need to set for yourself. Just that!

In the next chapter, we shall discuss the relationship between your intrusive thoughts and anxiety.

S3C8. Intrusive thoughts and anxiety

You would have experienced the following three states from time to time:

1. Anxiety without intrusive thoughts about your relationship
2. Intrusive thoughts without any accompanying anxiety.
3. Anxiety with intrusive thoughts about your relationship.

The above three states show us that anxiety and intrusive thoughts can exist without one another. Hence, anxiety and intrusive thoughts are not connected and intrusive thoughts don't bring anxiety. Let me say it again for emphasis in italics. *Intrusive thoughts don't bring anxiety.*

Think about how anxiety manifests in your body. It manifests physically. Anxiety is the result of the secretion of certain hormones (adrenaline, cortisol and many others, but never mind the names) in your body. When these hormones are secreted, you feel the effects in the form of racing heartbeat, perspiration, dizziness, heaviness in the chest, etc. These hormones can get secreted any time the brain thinks there is danger around, whether there is any danger in reality or not. So, when you need to speak in front of a hundred people, there's no real danger, but you may still experience anxiety because of this biological process.

Thoughts are a stringing together of words in your mind, in a language you know, and about a context relevant to you. You can't think in Mandarin if you don't speak it. And you can't think about your job role in NASA if you don't work there (except perhaps as a desire). What meaning you assign to this group of words in your mind is entirely left to your discretion. You give your thoughts the power. The thought may not have the power if you choose to not give it.

In ROCD, intrusive thoughts about your relationship get stuck in your brain. You have the power to decide whether you want to give them meaning or not. For example, if I get the thought of being able to fly, it does not mean I will begin to fly in reality. So, if I am getting such a thought, no matter how real it seems, I will not jump off a terrace. I will refuse to give meaning to the thought. Similarly, we can choose to not give meaning to the intrusive ROCD thoughts.

Sometimes the two (thoughts and anxiety) may co-occur and you may mistakenly associate the two as having a causal connection and create a relationship between them. You may believe that to make the anxiety go away you need to make the thought go away. That's where the problem lies. Since the two are unrelated, it won't work.

Think of your adrenaline gland as a leaking tap. It releases some adrenaline that brings about the anxiety. Now think of your intrusive thoughts as the result of an electric switch that is turned on. Your ROCD brain thinks that in order to make the anxiety go away, the thoughts need to be switched off. So you may try to turn the switch off. But the anxiety tap will not get turned off by an unrelated thought switch.

Since that does not work, and the anxiety does not go down, you may try to make it work repeatedly. When repetition does not work to reduce the anxiety either, panic ensues and that causes another burst of adrenaline to get released in the body, leading to more anxiety. This becomes cyclical. The failed attempt to stop the thoughts causes anxiety and the anxiety causes you to try to control the thoughts more.

If you recognize that turning off a switch will not help in turning off a tap, the connection in the mind can be broken. When you learn to break this connection, you can choose to deal with the anxiety and thoughts separately. Through the process of cognitive defusion, you can learn to accept the thoughts rather than try to push them away. Through mindfulness, you can learn to consider your anxiety as separate feelings in separate parts of the body and accept them as well, without trying to attach any meaning or build a connection.

Since anxiety is a result of excess anxiety hormones in the body, when the hormones get metabolized, the anxiety will dissipate on its own. Thus, if you internalize that trying to deal with the thoughts will not make the anxiety go away, you can learn to accept your thoughts and you will allow the anxiety to dissipate on its own. Understanding that the thoughts and anxiety are not related to each other will help in this process of anxiety dissipation.

In the next chapter, we shall understand the layered attack of ROCD.

S3C9. The layered attack of ROCD

Most times, an ROCD attack is not a simple attack. ROCD attacks in various layers, at various levels. When you first learn to use the principles of ERP to deal with your ROCD, you expect that if you stand up to Kay and decide not to do what Kay asks you to do, Kay will meekly shut up. But that is a mistake. Kay does not shut up. Kay gets more aggressive in the beginning. If Kay wants you to separate from your partner, Kay will do whatever it takes to make sure that you keep fighting with your partner and eventually separate from her.

So, when you first refuse to listen to Kay, Kay gets angrier and ramps up the assault. The assault may not just be with regard to the first thought. While you are managing the assault of the first intrusive thought, another thought might pop up out of nowhere and add more complexity. It is like being at war and being attacked from all sides. The enemy is not only capable of sending in more troops but also does not stop at basic weapons. The more you disarm, the more it seems to send. Look at the figure 3.9.1 that illustrates how thoughts may impact you from various directions.

Figure 3.9.1: Layers of ROCD

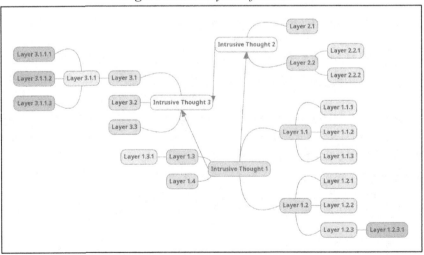

As you can see, not only can one thought lead to many layers, which can lead to further layers, but also, one thought can lead to a totally different thought, which can again lead to multiple layers. In the futile endeavour to attain certainty, you try to solve all these questions, in vain. But your ROCD is capable of asking more questions than you can answer. The race to find answers to all the questions your ROCD can pose keeps you stuck in the loop.

Think of Kay like a toxic boss. You are new to the job and your boss is toxic. He asks you to do his personal chores like getting him coffee, doing his paperwork, and so on. You know you should be standing up for yourself and setting boundaries but you don't dare to. Until one day when you pluck up the courage to stand up to him. He asks you to get coffee for him and even though you are afraid, you refuse to do so. If your toxic boss is used to mute compliance from you, will he take a refusal well? Will he just say *'Okay, don't bother, I will get it myself?'* No. He is likely to get angry and scream at you.

So, he says *'How dare you say no to me? I am your boss and you have to follow my orders'*. It scares you more and you comply. He wins. But suppose you decide to stand up to that threat as well and still refuse to get him coffee. He may ramp up the threats and may say something like, *'I will make sure you lose your job'*. That is even scarier than what he said earlier and you give in to the fear. He wins. But if you refuse again, he says, *'I will also make sure you never get hired in the industry again'*. Again, it scares you, and if you comply, he wins. But, if at this point you still refuse, you notice that he begins to cool down. So, you were trembling with fear but you still haven't needed to get him coffee and you have survived the episode and won the battle.

But your troubles aren't over yet. The next day again the same thing happens. He asks you to get him coffee. You are scared again. If you give in at any stage on that day, he wins and the equation remains as before. But if you survive the onslaught of his threats and insults, another day passes by, another battle is won. Then another and then another. Until one day, your boss realizes that you are not going to get him coffee and he stops asking. It is then that you win the war.

Your ROCD is like that. Say, you get the thought that your partner's eyes are asymmetrical and that you don't like that. The compulsion is to keep checking your partner's pictures to see if her eyes look very bad or manageable. But you choose not to do it because you know Kay is asking you to do it. So you get anxious but tell Kay, '*I don't care if my partner's eyes are asymmetrical, I still am not leaving her*'. Kay gets upset and more aggressive and says, '*Oh, but you deserve better*', and you begin to wonder if it is true. If you decide to check and do the compulsion, Kay wins. If you don't, and despite the rising anxiety you say, '*Yeah, maybe I deserve someone better, but I don't care. I am not leaving my partner*'.

Kay begins to fear losing control and gets more aggressive. The next thought is, '*Oh people will laugh at you, they will laugh at the two of you, and they will laugh at your parents*'. You are far more anxious than ever before but again, you respond by saying, '*I don't care if people laugh at us, I am not leaving my partner*'. Then Kay does not have anything to say and begins to withdraw, and your anxiety begins to come down. Battle won. Similarly, the next few times it happens, if you choose to stand up for yourself and your partner despite how anxious Kay's assault makes you feel, eventually Kay will stop bothering you about your partner's asymmetrical eyes, and you would have won the war.

Another analogy is the 'anger management' analogy. Assume that you are in an anger management class, I am the coach and it is my responsibility to assess you whether you pass or fail. To test you, all I have to do is to hurl insults at you and have you tolerate them, without getting angry. So, I start off with the most innocent insult I can think of, and you clear that without getting angry. So, I raise the level. I call you another name that is a little more insulting than the first one. You were not expecting it but you still take it on the chin. Good.

But I'm not done yet. I hurl another large, juicy insult at you. This gets you agitated but you remember it is a test and that if you tolerate my insults you will pass. So, you grin and bear it even though you do not appreciate it. But then I wallop you with a really vicious insult. By now you've had it. You get angry and you snap back. I shake my head and declare you as having failed the test. You continue to be in the class. Instead if you had held on just a little more and tolerated the fourth and the fifth insult, you could have passed the class.

Think of your ROCD in a similar manner. Your ROCD is the examiner. It attacks you with the first layer by saying '*You don't like your partner's eyes*', which you learn to tolerate. So, it attacks you with a more painful thought, which may be *'That means you are okay being with an ugly partner'*. Now you feel anxious but you learn to tolerate this too. So, your ROCD sends another attack your way and tells you that *'Your friends will laugh at you'*. Somehow you manage to fend that off too. But then ROCD sends like a really huge, disturbing thought that *'You will be isolated from social contact by your friends because of your ugly partner'*.

If you are able to handle this and not do your compulsive act, you win the battle at least. The next time, it will get easier. But if this last attack causes you to panic and do the compulsion, you will continue to be assessed on this obsession the next time. So, if you want to recover, the only way out is to fend off every attack from ROCD with acceptance even if it feels difficult.

These are the layers of ROCD's attack. For every layer you learn to manage, your ROCD throws up another and attempts to make you give in. If you can survive these layers by standing up to your ROCD and not doing any compulsions, no matter how anxiety inducing and difficult it is, eventually you will learn to manage your trigger.

In the next chapter, we shall look at the drug dealer analogy.

S3C10. The drug dealer analogy

Before your ROCD is diagnosed, you may have already begun to do some compulsions even if not too many or too severe - such as avoidance or distraction. But in the beginning, what seemed like a coping strategy possibly got out of hand soon and you may have noticed some dysfunctionality in your life. The more you kept it hidden or unaddressed, the worse it became, and began to envelope in its fold, various other activities. These activities may have been easy to do in the beginning but may soon have become difficult.

Compulsions are seductive because they do provide some relief in the beginning. For example, feeling that you have cheated on your partner for liking another person may cause anxiety and a confession may make you feel better. It is only when it gets excessive and no amount of confession seems to relieve you that you begin to realize that confession has become a compulsion that you cannot break out of.

Think of it like a friendly stranger you meet at a party, who encourages you to do some 'harmless' drugs. You do the drugs and instantly feel better. And the relaxed feeling makes you want to do more. So then you start doing drugs recreationally at first and then when you are extremely stressed. Then, you do them even when you are mildly stressed. You're feeling anxious about studies? Here's a pill. You're anxious about results? Here's one more. Feeling stressed over a break up? A pill is the response. This 'friend' has thus systematically robbed you of your ability to cope with stressful situations without the help of these 'harmless' drugs. One not-so-fine day you realize that you cannot operate without the drugs at all; that you're hooked.

Your ROCD is the drug dealer here and your compulsions are the drugs. You do them for relief in the beginning and you like the feeling. Then it keeps getting worse and ultimately you are hooked. By getting you hooked to the compulsions slowly and steadily, your ROCD robs you of the ability to deal with your intrusive thoughts without doing the compulsions.

So, this person (ROCD) who seemed like a friend in the beginning, whom you would rush to for help during anxious times is actually a selfish drug dealer who doesn't care about your wellbeing. He merely cares about keeping you hooked. The best approach for you would be to break off the habit and move away from him. But not only is it difficult to give up the addiction, but your drug dealer is also not going to let go of you so easily. So what do you do?

To give up the addiction, you have to acknowledge five things:

1. Drugs (your compulsions) are bad for you.
2. You can learn to cope with stress without having to depend upon drugs (without doing your compulsions) even though it is difficult.
3. The drug dealer (ROCD) is not your friend, but in fact, an utterly selfish being. When you resist, the drug dealer is not going to let go of a customer so easily and will try to keep you hooked.
4. If you must go to the dealer to get drugs (if you must do your compulsions), it has to be after you've tried everything, nothing has worked and you want some relief. Doing your compulsions is the last resort.
5. Going to the drug dealer is a step back. So, even if you have had to go once, you're going to try harder to not go to him again.

When you have acknowledged and internalized all this, you will stop treating your ROCD as your friend and try your best to implement ERP. You will not immediately rush to get drugs (do your compulsions) but do your best to resist the pull first. You'll give in only when the stress is unbearable. With repeated practice and enough resistance, your body will learn to cope without the drugs (compulsions). In this way you can slowly wean away from your compulsions and work towards your freedom.

In the next chapter, we shall look at the concept of ending the debate.

S3C11. End the debate

When you have an obsession about whether your partner is right for you or not, or whether your partner loves you enough or not, you inadvertently find yourself engaging in a debate. The question that your mind always seems to ask you is *'Do I love my partner?'* or *'Does my partner love me?'* Both of these are Yes or No questions. Your ROCD engages you in a debate about the appropriateness or inappropriateness of the relationship.

But in moments of clarity, not wanting to let go of your partner, and your partner not wanting to let go of you may be an obvious conclusion. However real your doubts may have seemed, you may have nailed down the irrationality of the thoughts and moved past them. So, there is no point in repeatedly engaging in a debate with your ROCD for the same question. Hence, you need to *End the Debate* in your mind.

When your mind asks you if you love your partner, you do not have to engage in the debate. You have to remember that the debate has ended and that you know the answer even if it does not seem plausible in the moment. Similarly, if your mind asks you if you believe that your partner loves you, remember again that the debate has ended. The Yes or No question is irrelevant, even though it seems valid and real in that moment.

Ending the debate is easy. Reminding yourself mindfully that no more engagement is needed will require work. When you put in the hard work through ERP, you will move forward in your recovery journey, by dealing with your obsessions without doing the compulsions.

In the next chapter we shall look at a way of winning the argument with ROCD.

S3C12. Winning the argument

Think back to when you have had an argument with someone. Not an intellectual debate, but a baseless, futile argument. Do you remember any? Who wins? I'll tell you who wins such an irrelevant argument. The person who didn't listen to the other side. Whereas the person who did listen to the other got so caught up in the other person's arguments that he believed some of it, tried to argue with some of it and got lost in intellectualizing rather than winning. Crude as it sounds, it is true. A baseless argument is won more by sticking to your stand no matter what the contention of the opposite person, rather than actively trying to win it with logic.

Think about it with reference to your ROCD. Your ROCD only likes to argue with you. And it wins because of precisely this reason. So let's see how it works in ROCD. The internal dialogue that you have with your ROCD or Kay is something like this.

Kay: What if you don't love your partner anymore?

You: No, I do.

Kay: Why do you feel bored when you talk to her then?

You: Uhh…does it mean I don't lover her?

Kay: Also, isn't that girl in your office prettier?

You: Err…that is true. You have a point.

The more you intellectualize, the lesser you believe in the relationship because Kay can present an endless number of reasons. As the German proverb goes, *one fool may ask more questions than seven wise men can answer*. So, you cannot answer all of Kay's questions anyway. This rumination may lead to further compulsions like checking, lashing out, self reassurance, etc. Kay wins.

Now consider a different conversation with your ROCD or Kay:

Kay: What if you don't love your partner anymore?

You: Umm…maybe. I don't care, I'm not leaving her.

Kay: But you feel bored when you talk to her.

You Yes, I do. I don't care. I'm not leaving her.

Kay: Also, don't you find the other girl in office prettier?

You: Yes, I do. But so what? I'm not leaving my girlfriend.

In this conversation, you refuse to take the bait. Whatever Kay is throwing at you, you are deftly evading by merely agreeing with Kay's words without agreeing with the meaning of the words. You are in effect de-fanging your ROCD by not letting the catastrophic scenarios painted by Kay get to you. You are choosing not to engage, no matter how real the fears seem. You are thus not only winning the argument but if you handle every attack by your ROCD in this manner, you will eventually even win your war with ROCD. This is how you can use bullheadedness to win arguments with your ROCD.

In the next chapter, we shall look at another way to respond to your ROCD.

S3C13. Agreeing without accepting

In this chapter, we shall understand the concept of agreeing without accepting. We start off by reiterating that Kay is a liar. Kay is not interested in making you feel better. Kay is only interested in pulling you down. So, Kay will always lie to you. Always! Kay may tell you that you don't like your partner's laughter. Or, that your partner does not love you anymore. So, you have a choice. Either argue with Kay and try to disprove whatever Kay is alleging through your intrusive thoughts or simply agree with Kay without accepting the meaning of the thoughts. What exactly is agreeing without accepting? Are they even different?

Let me give you an example. Suppose you are babysitting your nephew and your nephew wants to play cops and robbers with you. At one point in the game, your nephew holds out two fingers like a pistol and pretends to shoot you. *Bang, bang!* Since you are playing along, you put your hands to your chest and pretend to be shot. You act as if you have been hurt by your nephew's imaginary gun.

When you do that you are agreeing without accepting. You are agreeing to play along and you pretend to be shot. But you don't accept that you have been shot, you don't start panicking, and head to the hospital. The understanding that you are playing along in a game enables you to differentiate between agreeing and accepting and you put it into practice without even realizing it.

However, when ROCD strikes the distinction between the two terms seems to become difficult. You not only agree with what Kay is telling you, but you also accept it. Let us say Kay tells you that your partner does not love you anymore. You need to respond to Kay by saying *'Probably. I don't care'*. But when you think of saying it, it causes you anxiety. You cannot bring yourself to say it because to your mind, it would mean accepting that your partner does not love you anymore, which is not a pleasant feeling..

But you know that Kay lies to you. If you want to win over Kay, you need to lie back to Kay. So, you say it. You say, *'Probably. I don't care'*. When you say that, you agree with Kay. But you know you are lying because you *do* care. Since Kay does not need to know the truth, letting Kay know that you do care would mean you accept Kay's assessment. So, you agree with Kay's words but refuse to accept them. Since you have worked to end the debate, you do not need to accept them. Agree, without accepting and strip Kay of any power over you. If you agree and refuse to accept, Kay will have to beat a retreat sooner or later. This way you can systematically decimate Kay's hold over you.

This completes the section here. In the next section, we shall look at the recovery process in ROCD and what it entails.

Section IV: The Recovery Process

S4C1. Triggers in ROCD

We often say I got triggered by this or I got triggered by that. But what actually are triggers? Triggers in ROCD are those events that bring about obsessions, which in turn lead to compulsions and keep the cycle of ROCD alive. Identifying triggers will prepare us better for the onslaught of obsessions. If we can identify our triggers, we may recognize that we are going to obsess, which may lead to compulsive behavior. Knowledge of this can help us manage our ROCD better. Following are some ways in which triggers might be visible.

Sensory: Something you see/watch - movies, Facebook/Instagram post, videos, articles. It could be a specific color, shape of body part, or even a dress. It could be the texts sent by your partner too.

Something you hear - News of other people, podcasts, specific music. Or it may be the way your partner laughs or snores or speaks with certain pronunciations and enunciations. Specific words, names of people, names of books, specific music, anything.

Something you smell - Perfume of an old partner, body odor of the current partner, etc.

Something you eat - Food cooked by someone else versus food cooked by your partner, food that reminds you of your ex-partner.

Cognitive: A specific good memory with an earlier partner, a specific unpleasant memory with the current partner, or having an argument with your partner or even someone else.

Place: Specific places that you may have frequented in the past with your ex partner, specific places that you have always wanted to go to with your romantic partner but don't feel like anymore. It may be your place of work, where you see different people you may feel attracted to.

Time of day: You may find yourself more anxious in the morning or in the evening or on weekends or on specific days like Valentine's Day or birthdays.

These are some of the examples of how triggers may be identified. There may be many more ways in which your triggers may be activated. One simple way to identify triggers is to pay attention to the things that we consciously and subconsciously avoid. We avoid triggers because triggers lead us to obsessions, which lead to compulsions. So, you may find yourself avoiding places like a cinema theatre, a café, a pub, a sports ground, a hospital, or some music, or some foods, or anything at all. If you sit back and think about it you may find that you avoid them because they are triggers for you.

At the end of this course book and also in the Worksheets file, you will find Worksheet 10 to fill in your triggers. Fill them in. Examples have been provided to help you get started. Consult your partner to determine if there are any triggers that you have missed. Slowly, as you progress through this course book, you will discover more triggers, and deal with most of them.

In the next chapter, we shall identify the obsessions.

To-Do:
Fill WS10 - ROCD triggers

S4C2. Obsessions in ROCD

Obsessions are thoughts that cause anxiety, are intrusive and disturbing (Goodman et al., 2014). Obsessions in ROCD may take many forms. They may take the form of a thought. Thoughts could be in the form of doubts or questions. For example, *'What if I don't love my partner?'* or *'Is my partner right for me?'* OCD is called a 'what-if' disorder because there are many thoughts or fears in OCD that start with a 'what-if'. *'What if there is someone better for me out there?' 'What if I am in the wrong relationship?' 'What if my partner has stopped loving me?'* OCD is also called a doubting disorder and doubting is a standard feature of OCD. Any doubts regarding the relationship may be obsessions. For example, *'I doubt if I love my partner.'* Or, *'Are my partner's lips too fat or too thin?'* Or, *'Does my partner have a good sense of humor?'*

Obsessive thoughts may take the form of definite statements. For example, the obsession could be *'I don't love my partner'* or *'I should leave my partner.'* When definite statements become obsessive, people have a hard time as they believe them to be real thoughts. But they are still obsessions, because they cause distress. If you did not love your partner anymore and wanted to leave her, it would not cause you anxiety.

However, if you believe that your partner does not love you (without a doubt), you may either have low insight or you may be experiencing abuse, both of which you should not try to handle on your own and get professional help for.

Obsessions may be in the form of still or moving images. You may be bothered by recurrent images of your partner's perceived flaws. Or, you may be bothered by images of enjoying sex with someone else. Or you may get images of how awkward your partner was at your office party.

Obsessions may be in the form of dreams. Like all other obsessions, you do not have control over your dreams either. Thus, intrusive thoughts may make themselves visible in your dreams. You may begin to feel that your dreams indicate your real intention since dreams are considered to be a manifestation of your innermost desires.

Obsessions may be in the form of urges or impulses. For example, you may get the urge to break off the relationship. This thought needs to be distinguished from the urge to do compulsions, though.

111

Obsessions are not to be confused with normal day-to-day worrying. Obsessions are consuming, take up a lot of your productive time, may be sticky, and may bring about distressing emotions like anxiety, guilt, jealousy, hatred, or shame. If you are able to dismiss the thought that you may be with the wrong partner, it is not an obsession. If however, you do not want to leave your partner, the thoughts cause distress that you cannot handle without compulsive rituals, they are obsessions.

Obsessions also seem real. They do not feel like thoughts that have been thrust upon you. As if they are your own thoughts. As if you want them. You feel that if they were not real why would you get them? Yet, you also know that you do not want them. Otherwise you would not be struggling so much to get rid of them. There would be no ROCD.

Obsessions outlined in the Y-BOCS symptom checklist (Goodman et al., 1989 a, b) have been provided in Additional Resource 7 at the end of the course book. Read through them to identify if any of them seem similar to what you experience. Using Additional Resource 5 and earlier worksheets (2, 3, 4, 5 and 10) write down your obsessions in Worksheet 11, available at the end of this course book and also in the Worksheets file.

First, write down the name of your ROCD (such as Kay) in the space provided (Cell D4). Next make a list of all your obsessions. Observe your behavior and along with your partner identify what your obsessions are. Then convert your obsessions into statements beginning with '*Kay is telling me*' or '*Kay is asking me to*'. Complete this exercise before moving to the next chapter.

In the next chapter, we shall understand the concept of cognitive defusion for knowing what to do when the thoughts seem real.

To-Do:
Refer to AR5 - the Y-BOCS symptom list - obsessions
Complete WS11 - obsessions

S4C3. But the obsessions seem real!

What do you do when the obsessions seem real? According to the metacognitive model (Myers & Wells, 2005), people suffering from mental disorders like OCD consider having the thoughts as being equal to acting on the thoughts, due to the metacognitive belief called 'thought-action fusion' (Myers et al., 2009). You may think you have cheated because you get the thought of cheating on your partner. But that is untrue. It is like saying that merely having the thought of pushing someone off a balcony, makes me a murderer and I should hand myself over to the police. This does not make sense at all.

Cognitive Defusion (not diffusion) from Acceptance and Commitment Therapy is an important concept in the ROCD recovery process. Cognitive Defusion focuses on being more aware of your thoughts. Instead of trying to push our thoughts away, change them or fight with them, we may be able to learn to view them differently. Based on our apperception, that is, our sense making, the same stimuli may mean different things to different people.

For example, in the pre-Covid-19 era, the word positive had positive connotations. However, after the world experienced the horrors of Covid-19, the word positive in fact, developed negative connotations, where people were terrified at being diagnosed Covid-19 positive. That is, the word 'positive' was fused with being undesirable.

Thus, it is not the thought that is the problem, but how we relate to it. When we fuse with statements like '*I am a loser*', we feel bad, sad for ourselves or angry at ourselves. We judge ourselves, on the basis of our thoughts, instead of letting them pass us by, without judgment. Cognitive Defusion is the process of separating the thoughts from the meaning we attach to them so that we may be able to focus on things that matter. Defusion is a skill that allows us to detach from our thoughts and reduce the impact our thoughts have on us.

In ROCD, a big problem is the appraisal of your intrusive thoughts as real. When you get an intrusive thought, say, your partner does not love you anymore, it seems real, because you are fused with the thought. If you learn to defuse, you may be able to deal with it better. But you may think '*Since the thought is mine, isn't it me?*'

Well, you *are* thinking the thought but it is not you. Think of it like this. You are a body that is entirely grey in color - person 1 in figure 4.3.1. This is the complete you and only this is you. You have an intrusive thought, an automatic thought that pops into your head, which is black in color as shown on person 2. Notice that this thought is different from the real you, an addition to the real you. Notice also that it is possible to recognize that 'you are not your thoughts' and also possible to separate the thought from yourself as shown on person 3.

An intrusive thought is automatic. You don't ask for it, you don't invite it. It just happens. You that you are not responsible for getting that thought. It is like someone throwing a water balloon at you. You have no control over when it will hit you and how. So, you may choose to:

- Assign meaning to and fear the thought - *'I am having the thought that my partner does not love me anymore. This means I am unlovable. I don't deserve love.'*
- Try to convince yourself and your ROCD (or Kay) that it is not true - *'I am having the thought that my partner does not love me anymore But no. I am lovable. My partner will always love me.'*
- Try to mull the thought over in your mind to find a resolution to the doubts that come up- *'Am I unlovable? But I have always had friends who have loved me. Then why am I getting this thought? Has the love*

Figure 4.3.1: Cognitive defusion

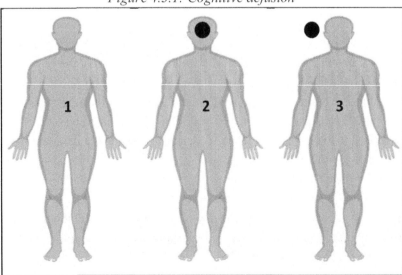

of my friends always been untrue?'

If you do any of these, engage with the thought and have an internal dialogue, it amounts to a compulsion and your ROCD will become stronger. So, when you get a thought that seems real, one of the ways to defuse the thought from yourself is to add two prefixes one after the other. Here is an illustration.

Your initial thought: *My partner does not love me.*

This thought is the automatic intrusive thought that pops up as a result of your ROCD. You can defuse this thought by using the first prefix.

The first prefix: *I AM GETTING THE THOUGHT THAT my partner does not love me.* Alternatively, you can say, *KAY IS TELLING ME THAT my partner does not love me.*

With this, you create a distance from the thought. This informs you that the thought is not yours but being given to you externally, by Kay. Once you realize this, you can add another prefix.

The second prefix: *I AM OKAY WITH getting the thought that my partner does not love me.* Or, *I AM OKAY WITH Kay telling me that my partner does not love me.*

Remember you don't have to be okay with your partner not loving you. You just have to be okay with the thought of it. If you have the insight, you know that your thought is untrue. This is how you practice cognitive defusion with your obsessive thoughts, without making you do the compulsions. There is an article that outlines the other ways of practicing cognitive defusion provided by The University of Sydney, which you can download from the link provided at the end of this chapter. Do try all of them and see which ones work well for you.

In the next chapter, we shall understand why we need to let the doubts go unsolved.

To-Do:
Download the article on Cognitive Defusion from
https://tinyurl.com/2z5k8yfb

S4C4. Possibility and probability

We do not need to solve all the doubts our ROCD throws at us. But it seems like the mind will not find relief until we do. There is intolerance of uncertainty which could be both prospective (I would like to know all the answers) and inhibitory (I cannot function until I know the answers) (Pinciotti et al., 2021). Your doubt about your partner's love for you may have been disproved time and again but your mind still keeps asking you, *'what if you are right this time?'*

For example, let us say that your partner has not been able to text you immediately after you text her. This may make you react in an undesirable manner. But after your obsession has passed, you may realize that you did not need to get agitated or upset about not getting the text on time. When you are triggered, though, your mind may ask you *'what if this time she is with another boy?'* The thought may seem real and Kay may force you to try and find the answer. So, how do you resolve this need to always know the answer and learn to stay with the uncertainty?

Let us understand the difference between possibility and probability. When we consider possibility, the only answer we can get is either yes or no. So, is it possible for me to win the lottery? Yes. So, if I buy a lottery ticket should I start celebrating right away? No. Because even if the *possibility* of winning exists, I may still not, since the *probability* of winning it is minuscule.

In ROCD, however, Kay might tell you that even if the probability is low, it still exists and that it should be attended to. If Kay is able to convince you of that, Kay wins. It is like Kay telling you to celebrate your win just because you have bought a lottery ticket. If you can tell Kay that you will wait until you win the lottery to celebrate, you have to tell Kay that you will worry about the disaster only if it happens and not attend to every thought that Kay gives you, since the possibility exists, but the probability is low.

In the next chapter, we shall try to understand why we still see evidence of our fears coming true despite knowing that the thoughts are untrue.

S4C5. Why the evidence then?

Sometimes despite being told that our thoughts are untrue, we keep seeing evidence of our fears coming true. When you think your partner has stopped loving you, you will begin to notice how her texts are not affectionate enough, how she spends more time away than she used to and so on. You ask why you shouldn't believe what your mind tells you. You have the Baader-Meinhof phenomenon to blame.

The Baader-Meinhof phenomenon, also called the frequency illusion (Kluchka, 2021), is a way in which our minds play a trick on us and we begin to see more of what we have put our minds on. Like, if a girl is getting married, she would begin to notice bridal exhibitions, wedding venues, honeymoon destinations, and so on. Or, if you are planning to buy a laptop, you may begin to see laptop ads everywhere - in magazines, in newspapers or on billboards. It isn't as if those cues did not exist before. It is merely that we begin to notice more of them when they are actively on our minds. Thus, we see what we seek.

The Baader-Meinhof phenomenon is dominant in people with ROCD. You struggle to deal with the anxiety your intrusive thoughts bring. So, you try your best to avoid being triggered and the Baader-Meinhof phenomenon kicks in right there. Because paradoxically, what you want to avoid seeing is more dominant on your mind and you end up noticing more triggers. So, even if your partner does a hundred things right, she would be ignored. But the few things she does differently (not wrong, just different from your expectations), you seem to notice more and consider them to be evidence.

The trick is to look at everything they do and not just the things they do differently and base your judgment on that. The Baader-Meinhof phenomenon is sneaky and takes hold without our realization. But when we do realize its occurrence, we can take active steps to disallow it from getting in the way of our relationships.

In the next chapter, I shall discuss one self-fulfilling prophecy typical to ROCD Type 2.

S4C6. Self-fulfilling prophecy

A self-fulfilling prophecy is the phenomenon where someone 'predicts' something bad, and ironically the person's behavior to prevent the bad from happening results in causing the bad to happen, thereby making the 'prediction' come true. For example, if I think my wife is angry with me for some reason, and I constantly badger her to tell me why she is angry, even if she is not angry when I first had the feeling, I might cause her to become angry with my constant badgering.

Now, no matter what the presentation, OCD always lies. The intrusive thoughts portend a danger that does not exist. For example, contamination OCD may tell you a surface is still dirty but it may already be clean. Harm OCD may tell you that you are a psychopath, but you may be a kind person in reality. Religious OCD may tell you that you are a sinner but you may not be. So, your OCD tries to convince you of stuff that is not true. Others may be able to see it, but your OCD may not allow you to see it clearly.

Similarly in ROCD, your OCD makes you read too much into innocent acts of your partner. If your partner is a few minutes late, you assume the worst that your partner may be cheating on you. If your partner does not text you right back, or in the way you want her to, you assume the worst again. If your partner has free time, it has to be spent with you, and if she doesn't or can't, you assume the worst.

If your partner is meeting friends without you, you again assume the worst and need to know whom she is with. Sometimes, in your attempt to find out, you may lash out at her. Or if you are triggered when you are with her, you may get her to modify her behavior to suit your wishes.

What impact could this have on your partner? As you can well understand, it may start with your partner reassuring you that what you are thinking is not true. But the reassurance may not satisfy you or only satisfy you in the moment and may make you repeat your unhealthy actions. It is likely that when your actions cross your partner's tolerance threshold, she may get annoyed and lash out. It is possible that she may feel that no matter what she does, she is not being trusted and may start resenting your behavior and your treatment of her. When she becomes resentful, she may begin to feel that it is not worth the effort to keep reassuring you of her fidelity and honesty. She may end up liking someone else over you who does not put her in the interrogation chair all the time, and she may cheat on you or break up with you.

This may seem like your fears were true all along. It may seem like you were always right in thinking that you may be cheated on or dumped by your partner. But, she may have been pushed into a corner and forced to retaliate by your actions. While not justifiable at all, her actions are understandable. Her action was a retaliation of your continued suspicion and lashing out or neediness. Your behavior created a self-fulfilling prophecy. It is this behavior that made your partner act the way she did. Being aware of this quirk of ROCD may help you in avoiding getting caught in this trap.

In the next chapter, we shall try to understand why being attracted to others is okay and why not being attracted to your partner all the time is okay too.

S4C7. Attraction is okay

Being attracted to others is okay. We do not have to be attracted only to our partners. We also do not have to be always attracted to them. Let us see why. We shall take the example of a cisgender female (let us call her Judy) as the ROCD sufferer. Judy has five men in her life - her boyfriend Tom, her brother, her father, a childhood male friend, and a male office colleague. She loves Tom, and has always been supported by her father, brother and male friend. Her office colleague is intelligent and she looks up to him. When Judy develops ROCD, her intrusive thoughts revolve around her partner's inadequacy. Her ROCD sends her the following intrusive thoughts:

- Tom is not as intelligent as my colleague
- Tom is not as much fun as my childhood friend
- Tom is not as strong as my brother
- Tom is not as supportive as my father

Judy struggles to understand that Tom does not have to be the best at everything. When Tom decided to get into a relationship with her, he did not use any checklists to determine if she was the best at everything that he wanted from a girl. He looked at her as an amalgamation of various qualities in different proportions that made her unique and dear to him. Perhaps he liked the fact that she had an imperfectly protruding canine. Perhaps he liked that she was not interested in politics. Perhaps he liked that her laughter sounded funny sometimes. He chose to like her with all her *'imperfections'*. Before her ROCD, Judy chose to like Tom with all his *'imperfections'* as well. Her ROCD has made her break down the composite and evaluate Tom only as the sum of all parts.

Judy's ROCD tells her that she should have a checklist of qualities that an ideal boyfriend should have, and she wants Tom to be perfect or the best at all the items in the list. But for a moment, visualize a music equalizer as shown in figure 4.7.1.

The music you play would sound cacophonous if all the bands are turned right up. All the bands need to be set in a specific order to attenuate the music. Similarly, what make Tom who he is, are all his qualities, good or bad. If Tom were to be the best at everything, would he choose Judy?

Figure 4.7.1: Music equalizer

What if he did not like her ROCD? What if he did not like her comparing him to her friends all the time? What if he did not like how short she was in comparison to him?

If Judy understands the way her ROCD works, she would realize that it is okay for her to like some qualities of other people more than she likes them in Tom. She may love her father more for his support and that is different and it is alright. She may love her brother more for his strength, and that is also different and alright. She may love her friend more for his fun quotient, which is again different and absolutely okay. Lastly, she may love her colleague's intelligence more and again that is different and totally acceptable. She needs to be able to tell her ROCD that even if Tom is not the best at everything, and even if she does love other qualities in other people more, Tom is still right for her and she wants none other than Tom, despite his many '*imperfections*' or inadequacies.

In the next chapter, we shall see how we can learn to grade our fears using the subjective units of distress scale - SUDS for short.

S4C8. Subjective Units of Distress Scale

Often when people are asked to rate the levels of anxiety that their obsessive thoughts may cause them, they may be unable to assign a number. The anxiety may feel too high and it may be difficult to ascertain just how bad it is in the moment. For this purpose, the Subjective Units of Distress Scale (SUDS) may be used. The SUDS is used to assess the level of distress in a systematic manner (Matheson, 2014). The SUDS is a simple analogue scale used to measure the subjective strength of the distress experienced (Benjamin et al., 2010). It starts from 0, which is no anxiety, and goes up to 10, which is unbearable anxiety.

For your recovery, so far you have listed down all your triggers, and obsessions. These obsessions will need to be ranked on the extent of distress they may cause you if you are not allowed to do the associated compulsions. For example, if you obsess about your partner's poor sense of dressing, the distress may be 7 on 10. But if you think your partner may be cheating on you, the anxiety associated may be 9 on 10. For smaller obsessions, the anxiety may be 5 on 10. Using the SUDS, it may be a little simpler to get an understanding of how to grade your fears. The SUDS has been provided for reference in table 4.81.

Table 4.8.1: Subjective Units of Distress Scale

0: Peace and complete calm.
1: No distress; alert and focused.
2: A little bit sad or distressed.
3: Worried or upset; still able to function.
4: Mild to moderate anxiety and worry.
5: Upset and uncomfortable; still functional.

6: Moderate to strong levels of discomfort.
7: Discomfort dominates your thoughts and you struggle to function normally.
8: Worried and panicky; losing focus and feeling anxious in the body.
9: Extremely anxious and desperate, helpless and unable to handle it.
10: Unbearably upset to the point that you cannot function and may be on the verge of a breakdown.

Remember that two different entries may have the same SUDS score and some SUDS scores may not feature at all in your list. It is not necessary that every entry will have a different SUDS score and it is also not necessary that one SUDS score can appear only once. Thus, multiple entries may have the SUDS score of 8, and none of them may have the SUDS score of 1 or 2. It is all fine, and correct. You will need to complete the exercise of ranking your fears in the Anxiety Hierarchy Worksheet when we fill that.

In the next chapter, we shall look at how your compulsions need to be identified.

S4C9. Compulsions in ROCD

Let us now see what kind of compulsions there could be in ROCD and how to identify your compulsions. Compulsions are actions (either physical or mental) that you may engage in to deal with the distress caused by the obsessions (Goodman et al., 2014). Compulsions can be recognized by the urgency with which you want to do them. A thought causes distress and the mind urges you to take some immediate action, either physical or mental. That action may be the compulsion. Let us look at some of the common compulsions that have been observed in people with ROCD.

Monitoring your own feelings and sensations: You may find yourself monitoring what you feel in the presence of your partner (e.g., Am I attracted to my partner? Am I aroused by my partner's body? Am I aroused by someone else?). You may also monitor if you feel 'enough' of a feeling around your partner (e.g., I feel sexually attracted to my partner but is the attraction strong enough?)

Researching and checking: You may start looking for information about relationships by reading articles, books, watching videos and generally excessively researching on the internet (e.g., 'What do good relationships feel like?' 'What are the qualities of a good partner?'). You may keep testing your feelings or your partner's behavior in various situations (e.g., 'Does my partner make me laugh?' 'Does my partner interact well with others?').

Comparison: You may begin to compare your partner with other people to see if your partner has the qualities you like in the other person. Or, the comparison may be to see if the feelings towards the current partner match or surpass what you felt with past partners or other potential partners (e.g., colleagues, partners of her friends, acquaintances or an internal image of an ideal partner). Or you may look at other couples and see how they are with each other with a view to comparing how your partner is with you.

Reassurance seeking: You may begin to seek reassurance about the correctness of the relationship. You may keep asking your friends whether they feel the same about their partners or not. You may consult with your family about whether or not they think you are in the right relationship. Or, you may consult astrologers, or fortune tellers to predict whether the relationship will last. All these are reassurances.

Neutralizing thoughts: You may try to neutralize a bad thought by replacing it with a good thought. If your mind says you want to dump your partner, you may neutralize the thought by saying *'I would never do it to her'*. When your mind says you may not love your partner enough if you have to be attracted to other people, you may try to neutralize the thought by saying *'No it's not true; I do love my partner'*. You may even try to recall earlier times when you felt and expressed your love for your partner.

Post-facto rumination: You may go over memories of some past events or situations to try and figure out the correctness of something in relation to the partner or the relationship. You may wonder whether your partner sounded smart enough, looked good enough with you, seemed to blend in or not and so on. Not finding the right or convincing answer may cause you anxiety and lead you to ruminate more.

Attempt to change your partner: You may attempt to change your partner's qualities, styles, or looks or have her do things just the way you want. It may be done angrily, almost as if to put the partner down about how she does not measure up. It is like trying to put your partner 'just right', trying to make her perfect so that she lives up to your standards of acceptability, regardless of whether you live up to hers or not.

Avoidance: Avoiding social situations (e.g., meeting with certain friends) or particular leisure activities (e.g., going to romantic movies, watching romantic comedies on television), or even fighting with the partner to avoid closeness are all examples of this compulsion. You may think that it is better to avoid the situation altogether than to get triggered and then end up doing compulsions. But avoidance of the situation is a compulsion in itself.

Proxy-compulsion: When you get someone else to do something for you because it would cause you anxiety if you had to do it yourself, it is a proxy-compulsion. This is another form of avoidance, where you would like to get something done but don't want to do it yourself, just so that you can avoid the trigger and not risk becoming anxious.

Negative self talk (NST): You may end up engaging in self-criticism or degrading self-talk (e.g., *'I am selfish'*, *'I am unappreciative'*, and *'I am stupid for thinking like this'*). You may even begin to believe that you are not good at anything anymore (even things not related to your ROCD). Or, you may have sexual thoughts about other people and brand yourself a cheater (leading to another compulsion of confession).

Distraction: You may try to push intrusive thoughts away from your mind by trying to distract yourself. You may either try to think of a happy memory or you may put on loud music to drown the thoughts or you may engage in praying or talking to a friend to make the thoughts go away.

You may have heard or read that one must not engage with one's intrusive thoughts and you may choose to distract yourself because staying with the thoughts may cause you significant discomfort.

Confession: You may develop a distorted view of what is allowed and what is not allowed in the relationship and think that everything you do may be amounting to being disloyal to your partner. This may cause you to confess your thoughts to your partner. For example, if you like how an office colleague smiles at you or jokes about, you may think you are more attracted to her than to your partner, leading you to confess to your partner about your 'feelings'.

Stalking social media: You may want to check if your partner is loyal to you and may end up stalking her on her social media accounts. You may want to check if she looks happier without you than with you. Or you may want to check if she is with someone else and probably cheating on you.

Lashing out at the partner: You may think that your partner is cheating on you. Or you may think that she is not spending enough time with you. Or you may think that she is not loving enough or not trying hard enough. All these and other thoughts may make you want to lash out at your partner despite knowing that it would probably not go well with her.

Apologizing excessively: This compulsion is common to a lot of OCD presentations (including ROCD), but it does not affect everybody. You may think you have wronged others and end up apologizing for the smallest of things. Often they are not even what others would consider mistakes, but you do. Sometimes it may annoy the other person for the number of times you apologize, and the other person may snap at you, which may make you apologize more.

Pre-planning: Pre-planning your course of action before entering a trigger in order to minimize your anxiety is a compulsion. When you are aware that you are in a situation where you are likely to get triggered, you may automatically end up planning how to minimize your anxiety if you are triggered. For example, if you decide to watch the rerun of a romantic movie with your girlfriend, you may plan to get up and go for popcorn when you know scenes that might trigger you more are likely to play.

Monitoring your partner's feelings and behavior: On the one hand, you may fear that you may be with the wrong person. On the other, the thought of leaving her for her imperfections may make you anxious. This may begin to show on your face and may give rise to another compulsion - to monitor your partner's feelings, expressions and behavior when you are triggered and want to conceal your anxiety. This is to make sure that despite you being triggered your partner does not show any indications of wanting to quit the relationship.

There may be other compulsions that you may be engaging in that may not have been covered here. Since OCD is a nuanced disorder, both obsessions and compulsions can morph from text-book presentations to something completely unique for you. If you have any compulsions that are not covered here, make a note of them. You will find the list of compulsions as identified in the Y-BOCS (Goodman et al., 1989a, b) as Additional Resource 6 at the end of this course book. Go through them and make a note of everything you go through in your daily life.

Using the previous worksheets (2, 3, 4, 5, 10 and 11), write down your compulsions in Worksheet 12, available at the end of this course book and also in the Worksheets file. First, write down the name of your ROCD (such as Kay) in the space provided. Next make a list of all your compulsions from the Y-BOCS checklist.

Next, observe your behavior and identify what your ROCD compulsions are. Then convert your compulsions into statements beginning with 'Kay is telling me to' or 'Kay is asking me to'. Complete this exercise before moving to the next chapter.

In the next chapter we shall look at understanding our compulsions from the lens of mindfulness and acceptance, using the compulsion matrix.

To-Do:
Refer to AR6 - the Y-BOCS symptom list - compulsions
Complete WS12 - compulsions

S4C10. The compulsion matrix

In this chapter, we shall further understand the importance of acceptance and mindfulness in your recovery journey. Sometimes you may think that your compulsions come without obsessions. Sometimes, the rituals become habits and you do not even remember why you do them anymore. Maybe if you think about them, you may remember what a ritual is supposed to prevent but often, the ritual is performed even without you realizing it, out of habit.

At times, you may not need to do your compulsions but you still do them. Sometimes, it is to make sure that there are no obsessions. You could stop them if you wanted, but you don't. When you are expected to face your fears, it means getting to a point where you do not do any of your compulsions - the ones you do not realize doing and the ones you do not care to stop. But facing your fears may have at least two types of roadblocks for you.

Unwillingness Vs Inability to Stop: Often your rituals may seem like you are *unable to stop* them. Whenever there is an urge, or even a feeling that this is the right time to do a ritual, you may just end up doing it and then believe that you are *unable to stop*. But is it that way really? Because if you observe your rituals closely, only some of them you may be *unable to stop* doing, because they may seem automatic. But the other rituals, you may be *unwilling to stop*. You may realize that there are some rituals to which you may say '*I can't stop doing this*' but what you may really mean is, '*I don't want to stop doing this*'. Those are your *unwilling to stop* rituals. Those are the rituals that you do realize you do when you do them or even before doing them. For example, checking and researching may fall under *unwilling to stop*, whereas neutralizing your thoughts may fall under *unable to stop*.

Unwillingness suggests awareness but reluctance. The state of unwillingness is a more mindful state where we are aware that the ritual needs to be stopped but we don't stop it, more out of choice rather than inability. The unwilling to stop belief is a more mindful state. Inability on the other hand suggests a total lack of awareness. The state of inability is a less mindful state where we are not even aware of the rituals we need to stop. The unable to stop belief is a state of not being mindful. The key skill that will help you navigate this quagmire, and will take you from unable to unwilling is mindfulness.

Transfer the compulsions identified in Worksheet 12 in the 'pre-classification of compulsions' table in Worksheet 13, available at the end of this course book and also in the Worksheets file. Write down UA against all compulsions that you are unable to stop and write down UW against all compulsions that you are unwilling to stop. An example has been provided in table 4.10.1a to make it easier to understand.

Table 4.10.1a: Pre-classification of compulsions (part one)

Example for filling in the Compulsion Matrix (Table A)		
Compulsions	Unwilling / Unable	Unpleasant / Risky
Monitoring your own feelings and sensations	UA	
Researching and checking	UW	
Comparison	UW	
Reassurance Seeking	UA	
Neutralizing your thoughts	UA	
Post facto rumination	UW	
Attempt to change your partner	UW	
Avoidance	UA	
Distraction	UA	
Confession	UW	

Uncomfortable Vs Risky: The second roadblock that you may encounter in facing your compulsions is that your mind might tell you that it is *risky* to face them. But when you objectively evaluate the rituals, you may realize that facing some of them is more *uncomfortable* than *risky*. For example, if you do not compare your partner to another good looking person, it may be merely *uncomfortable*, but not seeking reassurance may seem *risky*.

The word *uncomfortable* suggests that you could stop the rituals if you wanted but do not stop them because of the discomfort. Thus, you are aware that stopping this ritual may not result in harm, that is, you are more accepting of the situation. On the other hand, the word *risky* suggests that you think stopping the ritual may result in actual physical harm of some kind and may not accept that the ritual can be stopped. Thus, you are less accepting of the situation. If you think a ritual is *uncomfortable* to stop, you are more accepting of it than if you think it is *risky* to stop. In this case, the key skill that is important to develop and strengthen is acceptance. Acceptance will help you understand that what seems *risky* is in fact just *uncomfortable* and provide you the courage to face it.

In the 'pre-classification of compulsions' table in Worksheet 13, write down R against all compulsions that seem *risky*, and write down U against all compulsions that are merely *uncomfortable*. An example has been provided in table 4.10.1b to make it easier to understand. Having completed the above exercise, make the Compulsion Matrix as shown in the example in Worksheet 13.

Table 4.10.1b: Pre-classification of compulsions (part two)

Example for filling in the Compulsion Matrix (Table A)		
Compulsions	Unwilling / Unable	Unpleasant / Risky
Monitoring your own feelings and sensations	UA	U
Researching and checking	UW	R
Comparison	UW	U
Reassurance Seeking	UA	R
Neutralizing your thoughts	UA	U
Post facto rumination	UW	U
Attempt to change your partner	UW	U
Avoidance	UA	R
Distraction	UA	R
Confession	UW	R

Based on the intersection of U and UW, write down the compulsions in the top left quadrant. These compulsions are just uncomfortable and you are unwilling to stop them. So, in your mind they are neither dangerous nor automatic. From the point of view of facing them, these may be the easiest to face. You have both the acceptance and the mindfulness to stop them.

Next, based on the intersection of U and UA, fill in those compulsions that are uncomfortable and you are unable to stop, in the top right quadrant. Since these are merely uncomfortable, there is no risk in stopping them and you may not mind stopping them. You therefore, have the acceptance. However, since you are unable to stop them as they seem automatic to you, you lack the mindfulness to stop these compulsions. Hence, for the compulsions in this quadrant, you need to develop more mindfulness to be able to stop them.

Then, based on the intersection of R and UW, fill in those compulsions that seem *risky* and you are *unwilling to stop*, in the bottom left quadrant. *Unwillingness to stop* indicates that you are aware that you need to stop them and could stop them if you wished to. Thus, you do have the mindfulness to recognize that these compulsions need to be stopped. However, since they seem *risky* to you, you are not able to believe that stopping them will not result in a disaster. Hence, acceptance of the irrationality and of the ability to handle the consequences of facing the fears is missing. This means that for the compulsions in this quadrant, you are mindful enough to recognize them when you are doing them but need to build the acceptance to be able to stop them.

Finally, based on the intersection of R and UA, in the bottom right quadrant, fill in those compulsions that seem *risky* and you are *unable to stop*. See example in table 4.10.2.

Table 4.10.2: The Compulsion Matrix

Example for filling in the Compulsion Matrix (Table B)		
The Compulsion Matrix		
	UW	UA
U	Comparison	Monitoring
	Post-Facto Rumination	Neutralizing
	Attempt to Change	Self Criticism
R	Researching and Checking	Reassurance Seeking
	Confession	Avoidance
		Distraction

In the case of these compulsions, you will need to develop both the acceptance and the mindfulness to stop them. Understanding which compulsions require more acceptance and which ones require more mindfulness may help make the process a little easier. Table 4.10.3 is to provide the inferences about which compulsions would require more mindfulness, which would require more acceptance and which would require both to be dealt with. Fill in WS 13 on the basis of the example, customized to your own list.

Table 4.10.3: The Table of Inferences

Inferences		
U+UW (Uncomfortable + Unwilling to Change)	High mindfulness, high acceptance	Easiest to face
U+UA (Uncomfortable + Unable to Change)	High mindfulness, low acceptance	Build acceptance to change perspective on inability to change
R+UW (Risky + Unwilling to Change)	Low mindfulness, high acceptance	Build mindfulness to change perspective on the potential danger
R+UA (Risky + Unable to Change)	Low mindfulness, low acceptance	Work on both mindfulness and acceptance to be able to face

In the next chapter, we shall see one peculiarity of ROCD.

To-Do:
Fill WS13 - the compulsion matrix

S4C11. The peculiarity in ROCD

Let us now look at a peculiarity unique to ROCD. OCD itself is difficult to understand. Recovery is so nuanced that sometimes people may know what is to be done, but not how or when. Because as explained in an earlier chapter, the same act that you may do during the triggered state may be a compulsion, but it may be important to do in the non-triggered state. In addition, ROCD presents a unique nuance that I have not found in other presentations, simply because there are two directions in ROCD, which we have been calling Type 1 and Type 2. Look at table 4.11.1.

Table 4.11.1: Contradiction in ROCD

Direction	Obsession	Compulsion	Exposure
Me to partner	I don't find my partner attractive	Avoidance	**Saying 'I Love You'**
Partner to me	My partner will leave me	**Saying 'I Love You'**	Resisting seeking reassurance

In the first case, when it is Type 1, where the obsession is that *'I don't find my partner attractive'*, there is a tendency to avoid. You may avoid being with your partner, to avoid getting triggered. When your partner says *'I love you'* to you, you may feel anxious and doubt your love for your partner. In such a situation, the exposure is to say *'I love you'* back to the partner and sit with the anxiety that comes with it.

In the second case, when it is Type 2, where the obsession is reversed, that is, *'Does my partner love me?'*, you may feel the need to check if your partner loves you. So, you may do things to get your partner to express love. You may say *'I love you'* to the partner to see if you get the same response back from your partner. In this case, saying *'I love you'* to your partner becomes a compulsion.

Thus, if you have both Type 1 and Type 2 ROCD, you may sometimes obsess about your love for your partner and at other times, about your partner's love for you. The directionality will need to be understood and the appropriate response will need to be provided.

Generalized statements such as '*Tell your partner you love her as an exposure*' will not entirely be correct and may strengthen your ROCD if used incorrectly. So, extreme caution needs to be exercised.

Identify such contradictions now and if you find any, write them down in the Contradictions Worksheet in Worksheet 14 available at the end of this course book and also in the Worksheets file. The above example has been provided in blue as a reference point in the worksheet in the MS Excel workbook.

In the next chapter, we shall begin the process of creating the anxiety hierarchy which will be the most important document you make in your recovery process.

To-Do:
Fill WS14 - contradictions noticed in ROCD

S4C12. Anxiety hierarchy

The anxiety hierarchy is one of the most important worksheets you will fill in your recovery journey. An anxiety hierarchy is a list of all anxiety provoking stimuli arranged from the least anxiety provoking to the most anxiety provoking (Obi, & Oguzie, 2019). It is a complete listing of *all* your triggers, obsessions and compulsions. It provides an understanding of the breadth and depth of your ROCD and the presence of any other forms of OCD. It will need to be worked upon and updated continuously. It will be a tool that you will use for regular assessment of the changes in your thoughts.

Refer to the Worksheet 15 - 'Anxiety Hierarchy' available at the end of this course book and also in the Worksheets file. In cell D21, write the name of your ROCD. Next, map the earlier five worksheets and fill out the triggers, obsessions, associated compulsions and contradictions (if any) in Worksheet 15. The second column (after serial number) is Presentation of OCD. Note down all the presentations that you have observed in yourself here from Worksheet 2. The next column is Triggers. Under triggers, everything that triggers you needs to be filled in. Use Worksheet 10 to fill this column.

Triggers may lead you to some general obsessions, which you can fill under the Obsessions column. Use Worksheet 11 for filling in your obsessions. Use the statements under column 'Distancing from Obsessions' instead of the 'Obsessions' column. So instead of writing, *'What if my partner is cheating on me?'* write, *'Kay is telling me that my partner is cheating on me'*. Once all the triggers and obsessions are listed down, use the SUDS to fill in the SUDS column with the SUDS score. Look at each obsession and determine how much anxiety you would experience if you were disallowed from performing your compulsions to deal with the obsession.

These obsessions may lead to (or rather, will lead to) compulsions that you may do to reduce the anxiety you experience. Use Worksheets 12, 13 and 14 to fill in the compulsions, again using the 'Distancing from Compulsions column'. Worksheets 13 and 14 offer better insight so that you can handle your compulsions better.

If you see, one trigger does not have to lead to only one obsession and one obsession does not have to lead to only one compulsion. One trigger may lead to multiple obsessions and each obsession may lead to multiple compulsions. Also, some obsessions may be common to more than one trigger and some compulsions may be common to more than one obsession. Overlap is not only possible, but also highly likely and understandable. It is better to identify all obsessions and compulsions even if they are repeated than to miss out on some. This is critical to recovery, so that nothing is left unaddressed.

Your anxiety hierarchy is likely to be dynamic. Newer triggers, obsessions and compulsions may get added into it all the time, as you learn to recognize them. Older ones will keep getting struck off. As you learn to handle your anxiety better, the SUDS score for some compulsions that you have not even picked up to deal with may also change - it may go down. Your anxiety hierarchy may always keep changing. Do it well, follow it through, and you will see immense progress. There are some more columns in the Anxiety Hierarchy Worksheet. We shall look at them in the subsequent sections.

In the next chapter, we shall look at reorganizing the Anxiety Hierarchy.

To-Do:
Fill WS15 - the anxiety hierarchy (up to compulsions)

S4C13. Reorganizing the anxiety hierarchy

Now that you have populated the anxiety hierarchy up to the compulsions column, it will soon be time to bite the bullet and face your fears. The premise in ERP for the treatment of ROCD is systematic desensitization and not flooding. In flooding, you face all your fears at once and get used to them, whether you feel ready or not. You are not explained why you have to do what you have to do. It is more like *'I'm ordering you to do something'* rather than *'Let us discuss what you can do'*. It is a more difficult form of exposure. It can get overwhelming and may also derail the recovery process if not done well.

In systematic desensitization, the approach is more collaborative rather than dictatorial, where you are expected to face your fears systematically, one after the other and learn to manage your obsessions without doing your compulsions. When you face your fears, the anxiety that you experience should be high enough to make a difference but not so high that it overwhelms you into giving up. As you get better at handling the smaller fears, you progress to the larger ones. You decide which fears to pick first. You decide the pace. You decide the frequency. You decide when to start. You decide when to stop.

Think of it like resistance training. When you start off, the weights are small enough to lift without causing exertion or damage, but also large enough to exercise your muscles well. When you get adjusted to those weights, you begin to lift larger ones. Or think of it like learning a new language. You start with the basics, sometimes even the script, if it is different from English, like Mandarin or Arabic or Hindi. You proceed to the more difficult lessons only once you have mastered the easier ones.

In the case of ERP, you decide which exposures are easier and which ones difficult. You design your own course. So, you can sort the sheet on the SUDS scores from lowest to highest. We want to start with the smallest fears first and move our way to the larger ones as we progress. Reorganizing the hierarchy can help the recovery process to proceed in a structured manner.

In the next chapter we shall look at understanding the concept of mini-hierarchy.

S4C14. Mini-hierarchy

After the Anxiety Hierarchy is made, the real process of recovery will begin when you start exposing yourself deliberately to your lowest fears and resisting the pull of compulsions. As you get better at handling those smaller fears, you move on to the larger ones.

When you move on to the larger ones, though, it may still not be easy for you to face a large fear all at once. You might then need to make a hierarchy for each large fear too - a mini-hierarchy within the anxiety hierarchy. So that facing it does not overwhelm you into giving up. Let us go back to the example of watching the romantic movie in ROCD Type 1. If you find this extremely difficult to do, you do not need to expose yourself to this all at once. You may be able to work your way up to it by creating a mini-hierarchy within this trigger. It could look something like this -

- Look at a list of romantic movie names.
- Look at posters of romantic movies.
- Watch trailers of romantic movies.
- Watch some parts of the movie.
- Watch the entire movie.

So, while in the anxiety hierarchy, watching a romantic movie may be 8 on SUDS, breaking it down like this may help in facing the trigger eventually. These activities will obviously need to progress slowly and you will need to work your way up steadily, but with this mini-hierarchy within the anxiety hierarchy, you may find it easier to do so.

Similarly, in the case of the other example when you do not get the text immediately after you text your partner, you may get the urge to lash at your partner and demand an explanation. If this has a high SUDS score, expecting you to stop it altogether may be unreasonable. So, in order to help yourself manage it better, you can create a mini-hierarchy within the anxiety hierarchy for this trigger. The mini-hierarchy could look something like this -

- Wait for ten minutes before lashing out.
- Wait for thirty minutes before lashing out.

- Wait for an hour before lashing out.
- Do not lash out at all.

This way, you will keep putting a distance between your urge and action, thereby making progress, albeit slowly. This mini-hierarchy serves two purposes. One, it will make sure that you are making progress towards the ultimate objective of getting over this particular compulsion. Two, it is doing so by ensuring that you are expected to tolerate the anxiety in bite-sized chunks and not all at once. As explained in the last section, a little reduction at a time goes a long way in long-term progress.

In the next chapter we shall begin to understand how to schedule ERP.

S4C15. Scheduling ERP

Since you are going to start the process of ERP from the next section, it is important that you understand a small crucial aspect. Why this merits a separate chapter is that I did not want this important aspect to get lost in other chapters.

Exposure and response prevention is like setting time aside to study everyday so that whatever is asked in the test is doable. Mere response prevention as and when an obsession hits you is like trying to respond to the questions in a surprise test, without adequate preparation. To make this work, you will need to set time aside for your self-administered ERP sessions. You could start with an hour or even thirty minutes every day. But you need to decide on a fixed time that will be specifically reserved for ERP. That is a non-negotiable time, which you will not use for anything else but your ERP.

Doing your ERP session has to become a discipline like eating is. We eat three meals a day at specific times. No matter what happens, we are taught to make time for these meals. Similarly, no matter what happens, make time for your ERP. Your day's schedule has to expand to incorporate ERP. ERP should not be done when some time is left over from whatever your day asks of you. The rest of your day's activities should be done in the time that is left after ERP is done. If there are activities that you have to forego, let them be anything, but your ERP. So, in sum, set time aside for ERP everyday and stick to it.

In the next chapter, we shall rationalize an obsession of ROCD Type 1.

S4C16. Rationalizing in ROCD - Type 1

We shall now rationalize the first example mentioned in the anxiety hierarchy for ROCD Type 1. Remember that rationalization is always...*always*...to be done only in a non-triggered state and *never* when you are triggered - preferably with the help of your partner. Let us look at the example (numbered A, typed in blue color in the MS Excel workbook) in the Anxiety Hierarchy Worksheet (Worksheet 15). The trigger is watching a romantic movie.

When you watch the movie (or do anything else that you have been avoiding) to trigger yourself, remember it is like sitting with your face to the waves. You are mindful, and more aware that the wave of intrusive thoughts may hit you. This awareness prepares you for restricting yourself from not doing the compulsion and practicing response prevention.

Your mind may tell you that if you watch a romantic movie, you may get the intrusive thought that your partner's nose is too long. This obsession may feel real when you do watch the movie. You may then want to compare your partner's nose to the nose of the person on the screen. This would be your compulsion. You may compare noses, and you may either find your partner's nose better or worse. If you find your partner's nose better, you may get temporary relief but the doubt will not dissipate.

You may keep comparing the noses from various angles until you find an angle where your partner's nose looks worse and you may get anxious. Or you may compare your partner's nose with some other person's until you find one that makes your partner's nose look worse. You may be so critical and painstaking in the comparison exercise that you may indeed find something to be anxious about. Your belief that you are right about this obsession may get reinforced, and you may spiral into repeated compulsive behavior. Sounds familiar? So how do we deal with this? Let us take a step back and rationalize this obsession.

The rationalization process has five steps. I repeat and strongly remind you that the rationalization process has to be followed only in the non-triggered state. The responses can be kept ready for the triggered state but the process cannot be started in the triggered state. I cannot emphasize on this enough. In the triggered state, the reasons are not important. Logic is not important (Prudovski, n.d.). You just have to provide the response identified earlier and not try to derive the response through logic again. The debate has ended. I am repeating this over and over because it is very important. Let us look at the five steps now. For this example, let us consider the compulsion of comparison.

Step One: Rationalization of the Compulsion: This step needs to be followed in the non-triggered state. For different people, different kind of rationalization conversations may help. In Additional Resource 10, at the end of this course book, all the compulsions spoken about in the chapter on compulsions have been rationalized using one specific way in a simple to understand manner. You may rationalize your compulsions in the way that suits you. Particularly for this compulsion of comparison, the rationalization may look as shown below.

- Why do I need to compare? - To ensure that my partner is the best.
- Why should my partner be the best? - So that I do not feel like I am compromising in the relationship.
- Why do I not want to compromise in the relationship? - Because I want my brother to approve of my choice.
- If my brother does not approve of my choice, would I leave my partner in favor of someone else who seems better? - No.
- Does comparing help then? - No.

Thus, the compulsion of comparison may be to ensure that your partner is the best, so that there is no compromise being made by you in selecting a partner. In this case, the presenting fear (the obsession) is about finding the best partner, but the core fear is that you want your brother to approve of your choice. However, despite getting the strong feeling that your brother may not approve of your choice (your core fear coming true), you would not be ready to leave your partner for someone 'better'. So, comparison does not help. This means that doing the compulsion is a futile exercise because no matter what happens, you will not leave your partner.

Step Two: Mindful Acceptance of ROCD: This step can be followed in the triggered state. Acknowledge the following:

- I have ROCD and these thoughts are bound to be there. Accepting my ROCD diagnosis will not surprise me or shock me or disappoint me every time I have these thoughts.

- These thoughts are bound to feel real. I accept this as well.

Step Three: Distancing from the Obsession: This step can be followed in the triggered state as well. You can distance yourself from the episode by reminding yourself of the following:

- This is Kay's deviousness at work. Kay is asking me to give meaning to the obsession and to look for compulsions to do.
- Kay always lies to me and is only interested in making my life miserable, so I will not listen to Kay and I will not believe what Kay tells me.

Step Four: Distancing from the Compulsion: This step can be taken in the triggered state. The suggestion for doing the compulsions is given by Kay. Acknowledge that you again choose to not listen to Kay and will not do the compulsion.

Step Five: Formulating the Response Prevention Script: This step can be followed in the triggered state. In this final step, the essence of the rationalization exercise is condensed into the response prevention script. The response prevention script almost always follows a template of sorts. The response prevention script for this compulsion can be as shown below.

- If I do not compare and anything goes wrong as a result, that is, I realize later that my brother does not approve of my choice, I will handle it then. I will not dwell on it now.

Of the five steps above, the first step can and must only be followed in the non-triggered state. In the fifth step, as you can see, you are not only handling the obsession as it is but also preparing yourself for handling the core fear if it comes true. This completes the rationalization process for ROCD Type 1 obsession.

In the next chapter we shall look at rationalizing an obsession from ROCD Type 2.

S4C17. Rationalizing in ROCD - Type 2

We shall now follow the same process of rationalization for ROCD Type 2. Remember once again, that this rationalization exercise is to be carried out only in the non-triggered state, preferably with the help of your partner. Let us look at the example (numbered B, typed in red color in the MS Excel workbook) in the Anxiety Hierarchy Worksheet (Worksheet 15). The trigger is not getting a text from your partner immediately after you have sent one. The compulsion is to lash out at the partner and attempting to change partner behavior, making the partner feel constrained and trapped. Let us look to rationalize this thought using the five steps.

Step One: Rationalization of the Compulsion: This step can be taken only in the non-triggered state. Particularly for this compulsion of lashing out at the partner, the rationalization may look as shown below.

- Why do I need to lash out at my partner? - Because I think my partner needs to respond to my texts immediately and the way I want her to.
- What does it mean to me if my partner doesn't do that? - If my partner doesn't do that, it probably means she is with someone else and happy without me.
- Is that the only explanation? - No but my mind tells me so.
- Should I believe what Kay tells me or should I go with what I know for sure otherwise? - I should go with what I know.
- Is lashing out at my partner working well for our relationship? - No, it isn't.

Here, the compulsion of lashing out at the partner may be to ensure that your partner is happy with you and is not looking out for any other relationship. This would be the core fear here. However, such lashing out at your partner will only result in making your partner go farther away from you. So, lashing out at the partner does not help.

Step Two: Mindful Acceptance of ROCD: Acknowledge the following:

- I have ROCD and that these thoughts are bound to be there. Accepting my ROCD diagnosis will not surprise me or shock me or disappoint me every time I have these thoughts.
- These thoughts are bound to feel real. I accept this as well.

Step Three: Distancing from the Obsession: This step can be followed in the triggered state. You can distance yourself from the episode by reminding yourself of the following:

- This is Kay's deviousness at work. Kay is asking me to give meaning to the obsession and to look for compulsions to do.
- Kay always lies to me and is only interested in making my life miserable, so I will not listen to Kay.

Step Four: Distancing from the Compulsion: This step can be followed in the triggered state. The obsession was given by Kay and the suggestion to deal with the obsession to relieve the anxiety - that is the suggestion for doing the compulsions is also given by Kay. Acknowledge that you again choose to not listen to Kay and will not do the compulsion.

Step Five: Formulating the Response Prevention Script: This step can be followed in the triggered state. The response prevention script for this compulsion can be as shown below.

- If I do not lash out at my partner and anything goes wrong as a result, that is, I realize later that my partner is happy with someone else without me, I will handle it then. I will not dwell on it now.

Additional Resource 7 provided at the end of the course book includes the rationalization of all compulsions identified earlier. Browse through it and specific to your ROCD fill in Worksheet 16 available at the end of this course book and also in the Worksheets file.

This concludes the section here. The next section is the final battle with ROCD.

To-Do:
Refer to AR7 - rationalization of compulsions
Rationalize your compulsions in WS16

Section V: The Battle with ROCD

S5C1. The procedure

In this final section, we shall be getting into the thick of things. We shall learn how to do some exposures, and we shall also talk about a few ways to handle our compulsions. Since there is truly no end to the number of compulsions one can engage in, in ROCD, and since the manifestation of each compulsion is different for different people, it is impossible to cover everything one can do. So, I am going to pick up the compulsions outlined in this book and provide as many ways to deal with them as I can.

These procedures are not hard cast in stone, though. Also, core fears are different for different people. Hence, the procedure outlined in one compulsion may be used for other compulsions as well, if it works better. There is no one way to handle each compulsion. You should use whatever works best for you, provided you are using it well and not making mistakes in the implementation.

Before we handle the compulsions though, I want to explain how the exposure is to be recorded. First, since this is ERP and not just RP, as mentioned you need to set out some time maybe an hour for yourself every day to do your ERP. The ideal recommended time is two hours every day. But you can decide the duration that works for you. And you can also decide on what time is good for you. Do you want to do it in the morning when you are fresh? Or do you want to do it in the evening when the day's tasks are over?

There are different schools of thought on this though. Some people think doing your exposures in the morning is the right approach because you may be too tired at the end of the day and may have neither the willingness nor the energy to do your exposures. The argument against morning exposures is that you experience anxiety first thing in the morning and your OCD may threaten to ruin the rest of your day.

Strictly from a textbook perspective, this may be the right thing to do for two reasons. One, you get the most difficult task of the day out of the way right in the morning and leave yourself with no excuses to not do the exposures. Two, the thought that the rest of your day will be ruined is Kay's thought to stop you from doing your exposures when you are fresh and mindful. Under ideal circumstances, you should choose mornings to do your exposures.

The other school of thought is to do your exposures at the end of the day. You are already tired and stressed. Doing your exposures at that time may only raise your tiredness and stress by a few notches. It is like returning home from work and finishing a household task that may make you sweat further before going for a shower. Since you are already sweaty, doing that additional task may not be too much more to take on.

However, the flip side is that Kay may convince you that you are too tired to take up anything extra and *'how about picking it up tomorrow?'* The temptation to not add more stress can be high and you may not do your exposures at all. Hence, you need to decide what works best for you without letting Kay make excuses for you. Whatever you decide, you need to incorporate ERP into your lifestyle and hence, make it a permanent fixture of your to-do list, at least until you recover.

Next, the exposures are to be deliberate. Which means whatever your triggers are, instead of avoiding them, face them. Watching a romantic movie, looking at happy couples on Instagram, reading about happy relationships may all be triggers. When you are doing your exposures, you will need to pick out a movie and start watching it to trigger yourself.

Keep the Anxiety Hierarchy Worksheet open when you start the exposures. Remember to not take the most difficult triggers immediately, even though you may want to get rid of them first. Also, remember that you cannot afford to take too many exposures together. If you take the difficult ones first, or if you take too many together, you may fail more often and that may dissuade you from following it through. So, start with something small. Like say, something that has a SUDS score of 5.

Write down the date against the appropriate exposure in the Date column and start the exposure. When you trigger yourself, you will have obsessive thoughts about your partner. Note the anxiety that you are experiencing right in the beginning and note it in the Beginning column. Use the response prevention script formulated earlier to not do the compulsions. When you try to resist the compulsions, your anxiety will go up as it should.

In the Anxiety Hierarchy Worksheet, observe your level of anxiety as per the SUDS and make a note of it every ten minutes (or twenty minutes, if you find that more comfortable) in the appropriate columns. If you do the exposure right, after sitting with the anxiety for a sufficient amount of time, the level of anxiety will start dropping. Continue the exposure until it falls to half of what you started with. In the examples, you can see that the exposure was started at an anxiety level of 8 and terminated when the anxiety level dropped to 4.

Repeat this exposure over and over for a few days until you are desensitized to the thought and the associated anxiety is extinct. Move on to the other exposures in the worksheet systematically and keep eliminating your fears one by one until all the fears in the worksheet are ticked off.

The next chapter will be about starting small to recover faster.

To-Do:
Fill WS15 - the anxiety hierarchy

S5C2. Starting small to recover faster

When you do your exposures start with the ones that would cause you the lowest anxiety if you had to not do them. If the lowest compulsion in your list causes you an anxiety of 2 or 3, you can move on to larger ones. You could try picking out some compulsions that would cause you an anxiety of about 5, and repeatedly prevent the compulsive response until the anxiety comes down to about 3.

Remember that the objective of the recovery is to bring down the anxiety and not eliminate the obsessions themselves. So, it is likely that the anxiety experienced with ERP may never come down to zero. That should not even be the objective. If the anxiety is low grade, say 2 or 3, consider the compulsion handled and move on to the next one. If you spend too much time on bringing the anxiety down to zero, you may end up wasting too much time on one compulsion and derail the recovery process.

At the same time, do recognize that this process needs to be followed systematically. Do not take up more than 2 or 3 compulsions to handle at a time. Focus only on handling the ones you pick in a week and not all of them together. You may want to get rid of your ROCD quickly and that may make you impatient with smaller tasks. You may want to deal with all of it at once or you may want to deal with the biggest ones first. You may believe that if you understand the irrationality, you should be able to stop the compulsion.

However, knowing something in ROCD and being able to handle it well are two different things. If you take on too much, your anxiety levels may shoot up, overwhelm you and maybe dissuade you from working on your recovery altogether. Not being able to handle it may also make you pull yourself down and become self-critical. So, make sure that you do pick up enough to cause you anxiety that you can face, but also not so much that you end up giving up. Work your way down the ladder systematically, with the lowest being handled first and the difficulty levels increasing as the previous ones are managed.

In the next chapter, we shall understand the concept of in-vivo exposures.

S5C3. In-vivo exposure

What we have discussed so far about ERP, about how it is done, is called in-vivo exposure. In ERP, the combination of in-vivo exposures and imaginal exposures yields the best results (Gillihan et al., 2012). In ERP, in-vivo exposure means doing the exposures by placing yourself in the same situation that causes the anxiety to begin with. You may think that your partner is not good enough for you or you may think your partner may be interested in someone else.

In such cases, being with your partner in social situations may cause anxiety. In-vivo exposure is choosing to be in such social situations with your partner and triggering your anxiety on purpose. When you place yourself in a triggering situation, you get the associated obsessive thoughts and feel the urge to do the compulsions. The anxiety needs to be borne without ritualizing or doing the compulsions.

In-vivo exposures are more helpful if they are done in situations that cause fear and if there are chances of the fear coming true. So, if you are in a social situation with your partner where the members are only your partner's family, the situation may cause fear but the fear of your partner getting interested in someone else is not likely to come true and hence this would be less effective. Being in a situation with your partner's friends on the other hand may feel like the fear may come true too, and hence may be more effective.

So, placing yourself bang in the middle of situations that cause you the anxiety would be in-vivo exposures for you. If you are triggered by your partner's imperfect nose, look at it. If you feel your partner will leave you for someone else, encourage her to go for parties without you. Do more stuff that will cause you the anxiety that you have been trying to stay away from. Observe yourself and your urge to do your compulsions. Identify your compulsions and follow the five steps for response prevention.

In the next chapter, we shall explore another technique of exposures called imaginal exposures.

S5C4. Imaginal exposures / Scripts

Sometimes it is not going to be possible for you to expose yourself directly to your trigger. For example, one of your obsessions may be *'What if my partner is cheating on me?'* In order to expose yourself to the trigger in-vivo, since you cannot actually get your partner to cheat on you, you can use imaginal exposures. You can expose yourself to the thought of being in the situation. You can do so more fully when you are imagining it and that can prove to be very effective. You could think of the outcome of your partner's cheating, how it will affect your life, your self esteem and your relationships. Paint the worst scenario possible and expose yourself to it repeatedly to get habituated to it.

Sometimes, some fears may be possible for you to get exposed to in-vivo, but you may not be ready for them yet. Even for those, you can use imaginal exposures first and desensitize yourself to the thought before you take action on them. For example, you may be triggered at the thought of introducing your partner to your family because of the fear that your partner may not create a good impression on your family. In such a case, you may use imaginal exposures and create scenarios in your mind about the meeting going wrong. How your partner becomes a laughing stock, how that affects you, how your family scoffs at you for your poor choice - the worst it can get in your mind.

The simplest yet a very powerful way to do imaginal exposures, is through scripts. A script is a small write up on the worst possible outcome of your trigger, starting with your 'what-if' statements coming true. So, if you fear that your partner may cheat on you, your script could start with the statement *'My partner has cheated on me'*.

This is followed by what happens to you. Statements like *'We are fighting, my partner is laughing at me as I am crying and telling me I was never her first choice'* or *'I am crying and speaking to my mother and instead of understanding my distress, my mother is insisting that my partner has done the right thing because I am not good enough'* should be a part of the script.

As you may have noted, the statements are in the present tense and not in the future tense. Say *'this is happening to me'*, rather than *'this will happen to me'*. Second, also note that there cannot be an escape hatch.

Nothing that eases the situation is allowed to be in the script. For example, in the first statement, an escape hatch would be '*We are fighting and my partner is trying to calm me down and apologizing to me as I am crying*'. In the second statement, the escape hatch would be '*I am crying and speaking to my mother and she understands and is telling me I deserve better*'. Escape hatches dilute the script and render them ineffective.

Third, scripts are like every other form of writing much better if they show and not tell. Thus, painting a picture with words about where you are how everything looks around you, how your partner's perfume makes you go crazy as you hear the bad news, real names and situations would make the script more effective.

Sometimes when you write a script and read it back to yourself you may arrive at the core fear more easily. For example, when you write in the script that your mother is also not being understanding, when you re-read it, you may realize that it is that rather than being cheated on that causes you more distress. This is helpful as more exposures can be customized around this. You can edit the script and make this part more vivid and anxiety inducing.

Once the script is made, and you have edited out the escape hatches and expanded on what affects you the most, read and reread the script. Absorb the essence rather than just read the words. Make sure that the script is causing you anxiety. If you want, record the script in your own voice and listen to it on loop. After reading the script it or listening to the recording enough number of times, you will begin to feel desensitized to that particular trigger.

At the end of this course book and also in the Worksheets file, there is a worksheet (Worksheet 17) that will help you distinguish between an appropriate statement for a script and a statement with an escape hatch. Also Additional Resource 8 at the end of this chapter has two examples of how an imaginal script may be written.

In the next chapter, we shall talk about another type of exposure called interoceptive exposure.

To-Do:
Complete WS17 - the escape hatch exercise
Read through AR8 - the imaginal script examples

S5C5. Interoceptive exposure

When you are anxious, how do you know you are anxious? You know it through some physical sensations in the body. You may have breathlessness, palpitations, chest pain, choking, dizziness, tingling feelings, hot/cold flushes, sweating, faintness, and/or trembling (Clark, 1986). When you are anxious, you feel these somatic sensations but when you feel these somatic sensations, you are not necessarily anxious. These sensations can be the result of other actions in the body too.

For example, dizziness may be a symptom of spinning on a revolving chair for a minute. Or racing heartbeat and sweating may be the result of jogging. It is possible to induce these feelings voluntarily often enough and get habituated to them. So, when you do feel anxious and start experiencing these somatic sensations, you are better able to handle them. That is interoceptive exposure. It is the practice of inducing somatic sensations that mimic anxiety often enough to get desensitized to them.

Interoceptive exposures while highly effective are not recommended for everyone. If you suffer from epilepsy or seizures, cardiac conditions, asthma or lung problems, neck or back problems, or if you are pregnant, interoceptive exposures may not be right for you. You should check with your doctor if these exercises will be right for you.

While they are not dangerous, interoceptive exposures do tend to induce discomfort and hence when they are done, like any other exposure, there may be the tendency to avoid the discomfort. But, avoidance of discomfort will only serve to strengthen the fear and not deal with it. You will need to do these exercises over and over for them to work for you.

There are recommended times for each exposure and if you are doing interoceptive exposure, you should try to do the exposure for the recommended amount of time. Stopping sooner will be considered as avoidance. You should also focus on the sensations you experience without trying to distract yourself or do any other compulsion.

At the end of this course book and also in the Worksheets file, you will find Worksheet 18 that lists down the kind of exposures you can do to practice interoceptive exposures, along with the time for which each exposure needs to be done. Along with that is a space for recording your interoceptive exposures. Like all other exposures, set time aside for doing these exposures and record your progress. The more number of times you do it, the better you will get at handling it.

In the next chapter, we shall look at what a correct exposure should look like.

To-Do:
Try the interoceptive exposures in WS18

S5C6. What is a correct exposure?

In this chapter, we shall discuss what makes an exposure correct. When you have decided to get into ERP for getting your ROCD under control, you should also know the correct way of doing your exposures. Doing your exposures incorrectly will make you feel like you are working towards your recovery but your OCD will continue to stay strong. Following are some pointers on how to do exposures correctly.

Make time for other activities around your exposures: Have you heard of the financial advice *'save first, spend later'*? Exposures need to be considered like the saving part of your time. Do your exposures first. Do anything else around it. If you have two activities planned, one of which is ERP and you have time for only one, do ERP. If you must lose sleep, lose sleep. If you do not get time to eat, don't eat. If you don't get time to bathe, don't bathe. But do not do these activities when you should be doing ERP. So make time for other activities around your exposures and not the other way around.

Plan your exposures: Pre-planning actions to void triggers is a compulsion. However, pre-planning your exposures is not. Provided you plan your exposures appropriately. You have to anticipate the compulsions for a particular trigger and have a response prevention strategy chalked out. When you spend a couple of minutes planning that, you may be able to catch yourself before or while doing a compulsion and provide the right response.

If you miss doing an exposure today, do it twice tomorrow: Despite the best of intentions there will be days when you may not be able to do your exposures on a given day. The good thing about ERP is that you can do it as many times as you want in a day. So, if you have missed doing your exposures yesterday, do them today. Think of it as your salary. If you got half your salary last month, you will demand the other half this month. Just because it was not paid last month does not mean you will let it go. Learn to treat your exposures like that. Non-negotiable. Compulsory.

Don't pick up only simple exposures: Simple exposures are those that do not cause you enough anxiety for you to stay with. Simple exposures may be ones with anxiety levels of three or four. Doing them may seem like you are working on your ROCD, but they really create a false sense of action as they do not amount to much. Think of lifting five pound weights at the gym for a month and considering your workout done. Ineffective! Pick up exposures that are both difficult and manageable. They should be difficult enough to make an impact, but not so difficult that the overwhelming feeling makes you give up.

Do not engage in compulsions mid-exposure: When you engage in compulsions mid-exposure, you need to start with the exposure again. The value of an exposure is in the response prevention that follows. Doing your exposures and providing compulsive response in between is similar to wanting to quit alcohol but taking a few sips to take off the edge of the abstinence. You need to reset the counter to zero as soon as a compulsive response is provided.

Do not expect the anxiety to dissipate immediately: One of the biggest reasons why ERP fails for some people, is that they expect results immediately. When they don't, they panic that they may be doing something wrong, or worse, give up. As we have seen in the foundations to mindfulness, being non-striving when learning a new skill is critical to mastery. Being non-striving means not expecting immediate results and continuing to practice regardless of results. The results do show up but eventually. A mango tree does not bear fruit for ten to fifteen years. If one were to stop nurturing the tree in the first few years, one would not get the mangoes. One continues in a non-striving manner to nurture the tree, not for immediate results but for eventual gains.

Do not prematurely declare a trigger handled: After ERP has begun people come for subsequent sessions and tell me that they were able to complete the exposure and that they would like to move on to the next few items on the hierarchy. But they may have completed the exposure only a few times and not given it sufficient time to get habituated to it. The desensitization process is not complete with a specific number of exposures. Repeated exposures are required to make the anxiety come down and for us to get desensitized.

Decide on the scale of exposure: The scale of exposure is the level to which you want to take your anxiety as per SUDS. If you start with an exposure at a SUDS score of five and stop when it gets to six, it doesn't work. Decide that you would take it to say, a nine and then wait for the anxiety to come down to half that is, four or five. If you manage to bring it down to half quickly enough, move on to another exposure. If even after

45 to 60 minutes of exposure, the anxiety is not reducing, you may have picked an exposure that you may not be ready for. It is okay to drop it then and start with the same exposure when you are more ready.

Stop leaning on your compulsions: Before you realize you have ROCD, you begin to get obsessive thoughts that you do not pay attention to, but discover quirks that help deal with the thoughts. Soon, you begin to look at your quirks as your friends. Get an obsessive thought, do a quirky action. Feel an obsessive thought coming up, do a pre-emptive quirk. The quirks soon become compulsions. You just have to do them to make the thoughts go away. That is when they become compulsions, with you summoning them the minute you feel anxiety coming on.

But the process of recovery requires you to treat your compulsions as your enemy (see chapter on drug dealer analogy in this section), your last resort, in case you are just not able to tolerate the anxiety. And when you *do* do your compulsions, do them with reluctance, knowing that you have to try again the next time and not do them.

Let some compulsions happen: This is a controversial point and seemingly contradictory to everything else. When you get into therapy, the best thing to do is to not do any compulsions when you do your exposures. However, it is only theoretically possible to not do any compulsions at all during the exposures as you begin your recovery process. Most times you do not even know when a compulsion slips in while you are trying to do your exposures.

Of course that is wrong, but it happens. I haven't come across even one client who has not made a mistake through a compulsion while learning how to do exposures. If you end up doing compulsions, be okay with that too. Do not beat yourself down because you could not manage something that no one else with ROCD can either. But don't consider this allowance as a *carte blanche* to do the wrong thing. It is just an allowance to be kind to yourself for the slip.

Do the compulsion if you must: Again this is an even more controversial point. When you are doing an exposure and even after say, 60 minutes of exposure your anxiety does not come down, you probably have taken up an exposure that you may not be ready for yet. To bring down the anxiety that you are feeling, if you need to do a small compulsion, do so. I am going out on a limb here to suggest doing a compulsion but this too should not be taken as a *carte blanche*, a green signal to do your compulsions as you please. You are allowed this only under extreme circumstances.

For example, if your partner has gone out for a party without you, you may through great restraint resist the urge to text and check, resist checking his social media for pictures of the party, resist rumination if you have offended him somehow, and resist the urge to mind read that he doesn't want to be with you anymore. All this can be (or will be) exhausting. If in all this, the anxiety does not abate even after having exposed yourself for 60 minutes and you feel the need for an outlet, if you ask for a single reassurance, it is not correct, but understandable.

I repeat, do the compulsion *only* if it gets too overwhelming. You have probably bitten off more than you can chew and you need respite. This respite will help you continue your efforts and not give up because the whole ordeal seems unmanageably overwhelming. If by doing one small compulsion, you are still in the game, it is worth the minor slip.

Do not give up: Exposures are difficult and I will say this again and again. You will not succeed right away at everything. It will take time. You will stumble and fall. But as the Japanese proverb goes '*Nana korobi, ya oki*', which means '*fall down seven times, get up eight*'. So, all you need to do is to not give up. Keep pushing yourself to your limits, but in the journey, be kind to yourself. What you are attempting to do is difficult for most people. So, be kind to yourself while doing your exposures.

In the next chapter, we shall understand the importance of reflection after exposures.

S5C7. Reflection after exposures

After you have completed your exposures the next step is to fill in the Reflection column with your experience. This is the feedback to yourself about how your exposure went. Say, you step out believing that it would not rain. But it does rain and you get drenched. When you return, you reflect on the event and provide yourself the feedback that next time you would carry an umbrella. This would probably help you not get drenched the next time. Similarly, your reflection after exposures will help you manage them better the next time you do them.

You could reflect on the following questions. Was the exposure simple or difficult to handle? Was it too simple to help or overwhelmingly difficult? What worked and what didn't? Did you recognize your compulsive urges during the exposures? Were you mindful enough to not do the compulsions? What were the replicable insights you could glean out of the experience? How do you feel after the exposure? You may realize that you anticipated five compulsions, experienced six urges, could manage three and could not manage the other three. Thus, you prepare your brain to do better the next time so that you can manage all six.

Using this Planning-Exposure-Reflection cycle will help you face your exposures better as shown in figure 5.7.1.

Figure 5.7.1: The Planning-Exposure-Reflection Cycle

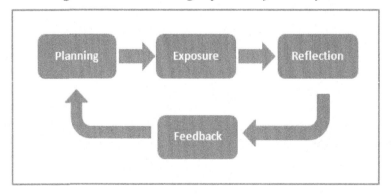

In the next chapter, we shall look at the undesirable but understandable concept of compulsions during exposures.

S5C8. Compulsions during exposures

Sometimes in the midst of our exposures, we end up doing some sneaky compulsions without realizing that we have done the compulsions. Again, it is impossible to provide all scenarios given the complexity of the disorder, but I shall provide two examples to offer some clarity.

Example One: You are watching a romantic movie with your partner as an exposure and trying to trigger yourself. You feel triggered during intimate scenes and you get the urge to compare if you feel the same level of attraction for your partner or for that hot colleague in office. You know you are not supposed to compare, because comparison is your compulsion. So, you respond to the thought by saying, '*I don't care if I am more attracted to my colleague in office, I will continue to be in this relationship with my partner.*'

So far, so good. But, while you do not compare your attraction, you try to neutralize the recurrent thought in your brain which tells you that you like your colleague more. Instead of comparing, you end up telling yourself '*It is not true that I am more attracted to my colleague in office*'. Or you end up providing reassurance to yourself by saying '*I am very happy with my partner, and the colleague in office is not all that hot*'. You did not compare, (which is the good part), but you ended up neutralizing your thought and offering yourself reassurance, (which is the unhealthy part). Your exposure was not effective because you did not resist doing *all* your compulsions. You merely replaced one compulsion for another.

Example Two: You are at a party with your partner and your partner seems to be enjoying a little too much with someone she finds hot. It triggers you to see her enjoying with someone else more and you feel the urge to lash out at your partner in front of the other man, demanding that your partner needs to spend more time with you than with him. But you know that would be a compulsion and you decide that despite the difficulty, you will not do it. So, with tremendous control, you paste a smile on your face and brave the evening with other people.

But, while you are not lashing out, you are trying to distract yourself by saying '*I don't want to think about it because it makes me anxious.*' Or you may begin to compare yourself to the man your partner is talking to and try to assess how you match up to him. Sure, in this case you did not lash out at your partner, but you merely substituted that compulsion with other compulsions such as distraction and comparison, thereby negating the effect of your exposure.

Whether it is neutralizing the thought and self-reassurance in the first example or distraction and comparison in the second, your ROCD would have succeeded in making you do *some* compulsion. Through some way or the other you are staying engaged with the obsession and hence the exposure is ineffective. If you start to mindfully recognize the other compulsions that you may end up doing inadvertently, you can learn to deal with them when they strike. Agreed, that you may fail in the beginning and end up giving in. But it is fine to give in and start again, rather than to give up altogether.

In the next chapter, we shall explore the concepts of reassurance, *deassurance* and coping.

S5C9. Reassurance, *deassurance* and coping

Let us now discuss the reassurance compulsion a little more in detail, as this is an important element of OCD (Haverkampf, 2017) and one of the most deceitful compulsions ever. First, identifying reassurance is difficult. Well, not as difficult as it is confusing. People are not able to understand the difference between what a reassurance is and what is not. So, let me first clear that up.

ROCD, like other forms of OCD, makes us believe that we are incapable of handling difficult situations, because over the course of its progression, everything seems to cause us anxiety and we begin to avoid triggering situations. We do not make an effort to handle the situation, and after a point we seem to lose the ability to handle any triggering situation. We choose to avoid these triggering situations, and we expect everyone else and everything else to not trigger us.

We expect not to be prepared to handle trigger words and so we expect that people around us should not use trigger words. We expect not to be able to handle romantic movies and so we expect that the actors in such movies should not say or do anything that will trigger us. We expect not to be ready for the world and so we expect that we should never see, hear or smell anything that triggers us. But as you can understand, that is not possible. It is like stepping out in the monsoons and expecting it to not rain at all rather than being ready to face the rains by carrying an umbrella.

So, when we expect that the world will behave appropriately (or proverbially dance to our tunes) and seek that confirmation from others or from ourselves, it amounts to seeking reassurance.

In the case of the rain example, if I ask someone '*Are you sure it will not rain?*' or if I tell myself '*I am sure it will not rain*' it is a reassurance. I am not depending on my own strength, courage or ability to handle the problem if it occurs. Instead, I am asking others or myself if others (in this case, nature) will do my bidding. How can anyone be sure that it will not rain? How can I be sure that it will not rain? So, if I am expecting that kind of response, I am looking for reassurance.

You may seek reassurance by asking people repeatedly if they think that your partner is ideal for you. You may see other couples who look better and get the thought that your relationship is not what it should have been. That might make you seek reassurance from your friends, who in their ignorance, wanting the best for you may end up reassuring you. You have completed a compulsion and you feel a little better.

On the other hand, if I tell myself '*I am sure it will rain*', I am not reassuring myself by hoping that the world will operate according to my whims and fancies. I am looking for certainty but I provide my certainty-starved brain the certainty of the other extreme - the catastrophic extreme. One of my friends has coined a word for these statements. She calls them *deassurances*. A *deassurance* is a certainty that is the exact opposite of a reassurance. Look at the following examples in table 5.9.1.

Table 5.9.1: Reassurance and Deassurance

No	Reassurance	Deassurance
1	Do you still love me?	My partner does not love me anymore.
2	I am sure my partner will not cheat on me.	My partner is definitely cheating on me.
3	There is nothing wrong with my partner's nose.	My partner's nose is definitely odd looking.
4	Is it okay for me to find other girls hot?	It is not okay for me to find other girls hot.

If you see there is certainty in the *deassurance* statement but the certainty is more about the uncomfortable scenario. There is certainly no comfort. *Deassurances* are used in imaginal exposures/scripts. Handling uncertainty is the correct response to a triggering situation but if you must provide certainty, let it be a *deassurance* rather than a reassurance. When you can build the courage to deal with the *deassurances*, you are coping. A coping statement for the rain deassurance would be '*If it rains, I will handle it*'. Look at the following examples in table 5.9.2.

Table 5.9.2: Adding Coping to the Mix

No	Reassurance	Deassurance	Coping
1	Do you still love me?	My partner does not love me anymore.	Even if this is true, I will handle it.
2	I am sure my partner will not	My partner is definitely cheating on me.	Even if my partner is cheating on me, I will

	cheat on me.		handle it.
3	There is nothing wrong with my partner's nose	My partner's nose is definitely odd looking	Even though my partner's nose is odd looking, I will handle it.
4	Is it okay for me to find other girls hot?	It is not okay for me to find other girls hot	If this is true and I still find other girls hot, I will handle it.

If you want to devise your coping statements, observe your reassurance seeking statements (where you expect other things to fall in place without effort on your part), turn them into *deassurances* (asserting what your mind catastrophizes to be true) and then add a dash of self-reliance to create coping statements.

People are also often confused between coping statements and reassurances because they think even saying '*I will handle it*' is self reassurance. The reason why this is not self-reassurance is that there is an element of self-reliance in it. When you say '*I will handle it*', you are not expecting things to not go wrong but preparing yourself to face the worst, if things do go wrong.

So, the rule of thumb is, if I depend on the situation to not go wrong or seek confirmation that it won't, it is a reassurance. If I am okay with the situation to go wrong and tell myself that I will handle it, it is self-reliance and hence a coping statement. At the end of this course book, and in the Worksheets file, check out Worksheet 19 which would help you to differentiate between reassurances, *deassurances* and coping statements.

In the next chapter, we shall discuss another sneaky feature of reassurance seeking that is rare but you still need to be aware of.

To-Do:
Practice WS19 - reassurance, *deassurance* and coping

S5C10. The trickery of reassurance-seeking

You know that reassurance seeking is a compulsion. Yet, reassurance seeking is very...well...reassuring. When your friends get to know that offering reassurance seeking is not in your best interest, they might learn to not offer reassurance. They may learn to say something like *'Your partner may or may not be ideal for you'* or *'You know the answer to this'* or *'You know you're seeking reassurance'* or some other deflecting statement. On their part, they are doing the right thing. In some cases, you may not be satisfied and despite knowing it is bad for you, still insist on being reassured. In some cases, you might understand that you shouldn't be seeking reassurance and try to stay with your anxiety without getting the reassurance.

Both these situations are not a problem. In the former, until you learn to handle the anxiety without seeking reassurance, it may be alright for your friends to provide you a limited number of reassurances. In the latter, if you are agreeing to stay with the anxiety without acting upon it, that's even better.

The problem really, is a third type of response. It is possible that your mind begins to look at any response which is not a confirmation of your fears as a reassurance. So, even if your friends say *'You know the answer to that'* or *'Do you really want reassurance?'* it may be already a reassurance for you. Your mind might tell you that if the relationship was wrong, your friends would panic too. The fact that they're not panicking means that everything is safe. So, even if your friends do not actually provide the reassurance, the response might still end up reassuring you without either you or your friends realizing it. In fact, not providing a response may also be a reassuring response.

The way to deal with this situation is to come to an agreement about how many times you are going to even ask a reassuring question to begin with. Restricting the number of times you ask for reassurance will automatically reduce the instances. This puts the onus of managing difficult feelings on you and not on your friends. In this way, you will learn to manage this sneaky feature of reassurance.

Educate your partner and family about reassurance. Let them understand what responses to provide when you seek reassurance. In the

Worksheets file and also at the end of this book, you will find Worksheet 20, which can be used to reduce reassurance seeking. Under each day, write a Yes every time you seek reassurance. At the end of the day, count the total number of reassurances and write them in the Total column. That becomes your benchmark to beat the following day. You should attempt to seek fewer reassurances every succeeding day.

With cooperation from your family and with the right follow through, you can reduce the number of reassurances you seek and make strides towards recovery.

In the next chapter, we shall discuss another sneaky feature of OCD called the backdoor spike.

To-Do:
Complete WS20 - reducing reassurance seeking

S5C11. The backdoor spike

One of the sneakiest features of OCD is the backdoor spike. When you get into therapy, you learn to handle these doubts. You also understand that your doubts are not rational. The fact that they cause anxiety is an indication that these thoughts are irrational. With sufficient exposures and response prevention, you soon reach a point where the thought of being attracted to another person affects you very little or not at all.

However, your ROCD may not want to let go. It may want to latch on to you for some more time. So, when the core obsession of being attracted to someone else stops causing anxiety, your ROCD may add another layer on top and cause fresh anxiety. Your new obsession may be *'Since the thought of being attracted to that new girl is not causing me anxiety, it must mean I secretly never loved my girlfriend. What if it has never been ROCD?'* Thus, the thought about not being anxious anymore about an ROCD obsession begins to cause anxiety. This anxiety has been called the backdoor spike, and is a part of Meta OCD. The backdoor spike is ROCD's desperate last ditch attempt to keep you hooked.

Just as you got over your original obsession by accepting the uncertainty and facing your fear head on, you also need to accept the uncertainty of the backdoor spike and face the fear head on. Just as you said *'Kay is telling me I am attracted to another person. I'm going to accept this uncertainty and live with the doubt even if things go wrong eventually'* you now need to say *'Kay is telling me I may never have had ROCD. I'm going to accept this uncertainty and live with the doubt even if things go wrong eventually.'*

Acceptance of uncertainty, regardless of the nature of the doubt is the only way out. Recognize the layers and stay one step ahead. Particularly for the backdoor spike, do realize that no anxiety is in fact proof of recovery from ROCD.

In the next chapter, we shall look at the concept of anticipatory anxiety.

S5C12. Anticipatory anxiety

Obsessions cause anxiety. Anxiety is the reason why you start doing compulsions. You want to relieve the anxiety and in the beginning, doing compulsions seems like a good way to relieve anxiety. But after a point, the compulsions do not seem to relieve the anxiety as well as they did earlier, getting you to do compulsions more frequently in every instance as well as more instances of it.

Think of an alcoholic who has taken to drinking to combat stress. When he first drinks, it may have been to relieve work stress, and a couple of drinks may have been sufficient. When that starts 'helping' relieve work stress, he may start drinking to relieve other types of stress as well. If he fights with his wife, he may end up drinking. If he loses some money in gambling, he may end up drinking. Even if he feels good about himself, he may end up drinking to celebrate. On every occasion, the number of drinks may not be restricted to just two but may gradually keep increasing. Slowly, he may get so used to using alcohol to cope that he may need a few drinks to just face a normal day. He may need to drink because he may begin to incorrectly anticipate stress even when the situations do not warrant it.

In the same way, you may fall back upon your compulsions to help you deal with the potential anxiety that ROCD triggers may cause. When the obsessions become more difficult to bear, you may begin to identify the cues that are likely to cause you anxiety and begin to avoid them. So, you may not go out on a double date with a couple you think is happier with each other than you are with your partner. The date may not cause as much anxiety as the thought of becoming anxious during the date may. This anxiety is in anticipation of being triggered on the double date. This anxiety is anticipatory anxiety.

Alternatively, when you begin to recover from your ROCD, obsessions that caused you immense distress earlier do not do so any longer. When this happens this may seem scary too because you do not feel the familiar physical manifestations of your anxiety. It may cause a mixed feeling. You may be on the one hand relieved that the obsession is not causing you anxiety. But on the other hand, it may seem like a time bomb waiting to explode and you may become anxious about eventually feeling more anxious than ever. Thus, even though the obsession does not cause the anxiety anymore, not becoming anxious when triggered may cause anxiety. This is also anticipatory anxiety.

Anticipatory anxiety may cause avoidance, and avoidance becomes the compulsion. You may take great pains to not have an encounter with the dreaded stimulus, because of the fear of the anxiety that it may cause. The problem with avoidance, as we know is that it causes a magnification of the problem and an overestimation of the intensity of the likely anxiety that facing the stimulus will cause. The longer the avoidance, the larger the problem seems to become.

When you start facing the stimulus that is the cause of the anticipatory anxiety (by avoiding avoidance), you may realize that the anxiety of facing the stimulus is probably lesser than it was in your mind. So, you might think that going on a double date may be a 9 on the SUDS, but when you do go for the double date, you may find your anxiety to be a 5 or a 6 on SUDS. You may be able to use this knowledge to boost your confidence and do more exposures to get over this fear altogether.

In the next chapter, we shall look at the concept of relapse prevention.

S5C13. Relapse prevention

Relapse prevention is not to be confused with response prevention, which we have been practicing so far. Relapse prevention is the set of processes that are aimed at maintaining the progress achieved during therapy.

When you reach the end of your anxiety hierarchy, and learn to manage your list, you have completed the most critical stage of your recovery. You may not have strong obsessive thoughts for a while. But just when you begin to relax, you may be hit by an obsession that feels as strong as always and cause distress. You may begin to feel that you have lost all progress and are back to square one. That is when relapse prevention comes into play. Let us first cover the explanations of a few terms that are relevant to the concept of relapse prevention.

Remission: Your intrusive thoughts will never stop. But if you are able to manage your ROCD thoughts with minimal symptoms, you are considered to be in remission.

Partial Remission: If you have moderate ROCD symptoms, but are still able to manage your obsessions without dysfunctionality, you are considered to be in partial remission.

Spontaneous Remission: Sometimes some people with ROCD may experience a sudden recovery and may not have troublesome obsessive thoughts anymore. It is rare but it happens. This is referred to as spontaneous remission.

Lapse: From remission, partial remission and spontaneous remission, you could sometimes briefly go back to a stage which may seem like your earlier unrecovered stage. You may be triggered and may not be able to help yourself from doing your compulsions. That brief return to symptoms, the aberration is referred to as a lapse. It is like having had one drink after months of sobriety. That is not a relapse. A lapse can turn into a relapse, if you are not careful enough.

Relapse: A relapse is the state of going back to pre-recovery stage, where you assign meaning to every intrusive thought and respond to it with compulsions. It is possible to go back from lapse to remission if one is mindful and follows the relapse prevention blueprint. But if one lets go after a lapse, a relapse is possible. A lapse is an opportunity to practice the skills learnt during the recovery process to go back to remission and not into relapse. Relapse prevention requires the understanding, internalization and practice of a few concepts that we have discussed earlier.

Exposures: Identify everything that triggers the thoughts and make sure you expose yourself to it. Exposures can be deliberate exposures or accidental exposures. Deliberate exposures are when you create time for the exposures and schedule them in your day. This is the best way to practice exposures. Accidental exposures are when you are exposed to some trigger without wanting to. In this case, do not avoid. Face the triggers and prevent the compulsive response.

Mindfulness: If you practice mindfulness, you may be able to catch yourself in the midst of a lapse and work your way back into remission from there. Being mindful can potentially prevent the slide back into a relapse.

Acceptance: Being aware of a lapse and accepting that you are not in remission anymore is an important realization to have. Accepting that the lapse may lead to relapse is important. Accepting that you may have to go through the rigor of ERP again is also important. If you have the insight and you accept these possibilities in case of a lapse, you may be successful in preventing a relapse.

Compassion: It is understandable to be frustrated to have the symptoms returning when you thought that the worst is behind you. Along with the lapse in symptoms, you may lapse into self-criticism too. You may begin to think that the lapse is your fault. At this moment, practicing self-compassion is important. It was not your fault that you got ROCD to begin with. And it is not your fault that your symptoms are coming back. If you begin to be critical of yourself and lose hope you may end up inviting a relapse.

Whether you lapse or relapse, do remember that it is not your fault. Many sufferers relapse because it is common in ROCD. However, you also know what needs to be done to return to remission. If required, go through the course book again and keep practicing. It will definitely not be as difficult as it was the first time. If you could do it then, you can do it again.

The next chapter will be the conclusion of this course book.

S5C14. Conclusion

This is the last chapter of this course book. Thank you for making it this far. In this chapter, I am just going to leave you with a few thoughts. If you have followed this course book through, you may be able to get a grip of your ROCD to a large extent. However, ROCD, or any other presentation of OCD is so nuanced that sometimes the same concept may need to be explained in various different ways, from various different angles, and with various analogies and metaphors before it is well understood and implemented. I know various books have been written about dealing with OCD at home, but I am always amazed at the peripheral text book approach. Beyond just the amazement, I am also worried about the incorrect interpretation and implementation.

Through the course of my practice, I have devised certain methods that work well. Through this course book, I have tried to offer those methods to you. However, this course book does not replace therapy and if this course book does not seem to help do not follow it blindly. If you do not understand the language or if the concepts are confusing, do not assume that whatever you understand may be enough and continue practicing blindly. Read and re-read and between your partner and you, try to understand the concepts well before trying to implement them. In case you still do not understand, reach out to me at sunil.punjabi@unshackle.in and I shall endeavor to resolve your doubts.

There is another aspect that I have wanted to cover but have hesitated to mention because it offends people with OCD. I know it is not palatable when people who do not understand OCD, use it as an adjective. I have seen people say '*I am so OCD, I need to keep my desk clean*' or something similar. To them I say, '*I am so brain tumor because I get headaches*'.

But I have something different to say to you. I know it can be offending, but try not to take offence. You may try to correct people's misunderstanding, but try not to make it an object of your indignation to make them agree, because your indignation goes against the concept of acceptance. To the ones who do not understand, it does not matter. When you get annoyed, they may either listen to you or they may not. Especially entitled people who revel in troubling others may consider this as a weapon to be used against you every time you are triggered. So, let it go. Your annoyance is not teaching them a lesson. It is only upsetting you and impeding your recovery process.

Similarly, when there is a reference to a game or quiz in OCD, even with legitimate questions, you may get offended because to you OCD is not a game. Once again, I agree. OCD is not a game. But when you see any such game, quiz, comic, coffee shop, or anything that replaces one word in OCD and uses the acronym, make a practice to let it slide. I have come across promotions such as Obsessive Christmas Disorder and Obsessive Coffee Disorder and it is no doubt annoying. But it is not your baton to carry if it is going to stand in the way of your recovery.

You have enough problems in your own life and you do not need the additional burden of having to become an activist to educate the world about how debilitating your disorder is. At least not right now. Your energy could be better spent in working towards your recovery first and then picking up the charge of educating others.

Do realize that I am not proposing dropping the education part, because it is critical if awareness of OCD has to be increased. But I am merely suggesting a reversal in priority for now. Work on your recovery first. Let nothing come in the way. Not even the need to increase awareness. Trying to increase awareness when you recover will come from a position of strength. Trying to increase awareness when you are struggling will seem like petulance and will also take you further away from your recovery.

Now you are armed. Go forth and conquer!

Additional Resources

ADDITIONAL RESOURCES

Additional Resource 1: Limit of Liability / Disclaimer of Warranty

The author, and anyone else involved in creating this course book make no representations or warranties with respect to the completeness of the contents of this work and specifically disclaim all warranties, including without limitation warranties of fitness for every situation, despite best efforts to make the work exhaustive. This work does not purport to replace professional help, but can act as an adjunct to professional help. If professional help is required or if the course book does not adequately cover the individual requirements, the services of a professional therapist should be sought. Neither the author nor anyone else involved in the course book shall be liable for damages arising from incorrect use of the strategies and techniques outlined in the course book.

Certain websites or books or other sources of information may be mentioned in this course book. However, this does not mean that the author or anyone else involved in the creation of this course book endorse in perpetuity the information such sources may provide or the recommendations they may make. Further, such sources may have been altered or pulled down between the time this course book was created and when it is used. The author and anyone else involved in creating the course book do not take any responsibility for making sure that such information is made available.

While the author will try to update the content in this work regularly, medical disorders like OCD change form frequently and therefore, some information may seem incomplete and may contain some inaccuracies or typographical errors, which may remain uncorrected due to oversight. The author and anyone else involved in creating this course book shall not be liable for damages due to such oversight.

Whom is this course book NOT for?

This is a course book for people who have OCD, specifically, ROCD. If you have OCD, or you are a caregiver of someone with OCD, you will benefit from this course book. If you specifically have ROCD, or you are the partner and/or caregiver of someone with ROCD, you will benefit more from this course book.

However, you may not benefit from this course book if you are indeed in a toxic relationship. It is critical to make sure you either get the right diagnosis or understand your symptoms clearly enough to accurately diagnose yourself with ROCD without a shadow of doubt. If you are in a toxic relationship, this course book may not be of help to you.

Further, if you have co-morbidities (other disorders along with OCD) that require medicinal intervention, and you are resisting that, this course book may not be of help you. Many co-morbid disorders are possible with OCD and if any of those stand in the way, you may not benefit. For example, if there is depression along with ROCD, and your depression disallows you to follow the process through, running through the course book cursorily will not benefit you. This course book may also not help you if the severity of your ROCD is high. No course or book can replace professional real-time help in that case. You may need a combination of medicines and therapy if your ROCD is severe.

Other than that, if you have the right attitude for beating your ROCD and are willing to put in the effort, this course book will definitely help you in your recovery process.

Client Details Form

I have read the Disclaimer and I agree with it (Yes/No)

Your name: _____

Your email ID: _____

Your partner's name: _____

Your partner's email ID: _____

Your age: _____   Your partner's age: _____

Do either you or your partner suffer from ROCD? (Yes/No)

If yes, who does? (Me/My partner): _____

Would you like to be contacted for future updates? (Yes/No)

Additional Resource 2: Progressive Muscle Relaxation

Progressive Muscle Relaxation Links
Female Guide: https://youtu.be/86HUcX8ZtAk
Male Guide: https://www.youtu.be/R0L-4bRY2pM

The method to clench specific muscle groups in PMR taken from the University of Michigan Health Website

Muscle group	What to do
Hands	Clench them.
Wrists and forearms	Extend them, and bend your hands back at the wrist.
Biceps and upper arms	Clench your hands into fists, bend your arms at the elbows, and flex your biceps.
Shoulders	Shrug them (raise toward your ears).
Forehead	Wrinkle it into a deep frown.
Around the eyes and bridge of the nose	Close your eyes as tightly as you can. (Remove contact lenses before you start the exercise).
Cheeks and jaws	Smile as widely as you can.
Around the mouth	Press your lips together tightly. (Check your face for tension).
Back of the neck	Press the back of your head against the floor or chair.
Front of the neck	Touch your chin to your chest. (Try not to create tension in your neck and head).
Chest	Take a deep breath, and hold it for 4 to 10 seconds.
Back	Arch your back up and away from the floor or chair.
Stomach	Suck it into a tight knot. (Check your chest and stomach for tension).
Hips and buttocks	Press your buttocks together tightly.
Thighs	Clench them hard.
Lower legs	Point your toes toward your face. Then point your toes away, and curl them downward at the same time. (Check the area from your waist down for tension).

Additional Resource 3: 23 Tips to Sleep Better

We do not realize, but most of us do not get adequate sleep. Either the quantity is insufficient, or the quality is bad, or both. We like to believe that we can do with very little sleep. Or that we can make up for it, if needed. Our minds have been corrupted on this issue with stories of world leaders and successful people making do with fewer hours of sleep. People like Narendra Modi, Barrack Obama and Shah Rukh Khan claim to sleep for only four hours a day. As a result, we may have begun to believe that less sleep equals to success. But Margaret Thatcher, who also slept for not more than 4 hours per day, died of Alzheimer's disease, which is associated with poor sleeping habits.

It is borne out by research that the human body needs on an average, seven hours of sleep a day. Some people may need eight hours, and some may need six, but believing that you can make do with fewer hours of sleep than that is a recipe for ill-health.

Some people want to get good sleep but are unable to. They toss and turn in their beds, sleep late and their whole cycle is disturbed. They feel lethargic throughout the day, find themselves nodding off during meetings or drag themselves to do any physical activity (or altogether avoid it if they can help it).

Sleep is one of the most important requirements for maintaining good physical and mental health. Poor sleep can lead to or worsen many physical and mental ailments. We may also know what we need to do to get better sleep but we still end up not doing it. In the hope that this article will encourage some readers to look at sleep a little more considerately, here are 23 simple tips for better sleep.

1. A comfortable bed, bedding and pillow: Make sure that the bed that you are sleeping in is clean and comfortable. The mattress should be comfortable, and there should be no bedbugs (obviously). Make sure that the bedding and blanket you are using are soft, comfortable and clean, with no unpleasant odors. Make sure that the pillow you use is of the right thickness so as to keep your neck straight, to avoid any aches and pains due to uncomfortable sleep posture.

2. Avoid sleeping in a room with the light on: The human circadian rhythm develops on the basis of light and dark parts of the day. The circadian rhythm is like a built-in alarm clock that lets your body know it is time to sleep when it is dark, and it is time to stay awake when it is bright. Trying to sleep in a room that is not dark can disrupt the circadian rhythm and affect the quality of sleep. Make sure that the room is dark or use an eye mask in a room that is not dark.

3. Sleep in a quiet room: It is difficult to sleep in a room where there is noise and it also affects the quality of sleep. Make sure that when you are trying to sleep, the room is as quiet as you can make it. If you try to sleep, while someone else is watching TV in the same room, it will definitely affect the quality of your sleep.

4. Sleep in ambient temperature: Sleeping in a room that is either too hot or too cold can affect the quality of sleep. The agreeable temperature can be different for different people, and hence there is no benchmark to follow. In the US and UK, the agreeable temperature is said to be between 18 and 20 degrees Celsius, but in India, it could be different. Make sure that the temperature in your room is right for you.

5. Use pleasant aromas: In recent times, aromatic oils like lavender have been used for relaxation purposes. Lavender oil has also been suggested for relieving anxiety and depression. Using it in your room for mild fragrance can be soothing and help you sleep better.

6. Don't eat anything heavy before sleeping: Eating heavy food right before sleeping can disrupt your digestion, generate acidity in the stomach and affect your sleep.

7. Avoid caffeine before sleeping: Most of us have used caffeine to keep us awake when we have an exam or a presentation the following day. Caffeine is a stimulant and delays the body clock, so it is harder for us to fall asleep with caffeine in our body. Hence use of caffeine should be avoided before sleep.

8. Avoid sugar: Consumption of sugar, particularly refined sugar, is associated with poor sleep. In addition to harmful effects like obesity and sugar addiction, excessive sugar consumption can also lead to 'sugar rush' that disturbs the body clock and interferes with sleep. Hence, sugar should also be avoided before sleep.

9. Avoid alcohol to induce sleep: Although alcohol can cause drowsiness, giving the illusion that it aids sleep, it actually affects sleep quality. As a result, a person may not be able to sleep unless he has a nightcap, leading to a much larger problem. Using alcohol to fall asleep is not a solution.

10. Cut down liquid intake before sleeping: Consuming liquids may cause nocturia, which is excessive urination at night. It can not only adversely affect sleep at night, but also make you feel drowsy in the day time. Also, it is advisable to use the washroom to relieve yourself before hitting the bed, to further reduce the chances of needing to go.

11. Take a relaxing bath: Bathing in the evening before sleeping can induce relaxation and will help you sleep better. Research shows that bathing before sleeping can improve the overall quality of sleep and also help you sleep longer.

12. Avoid exposure to blue light: Blue light from gadgets hampers sleep. It is strongly recommended to not use gadgets such as smartphones, tabs, and laptops before bedtime. This affects the circadian rhythm and makes it difficult to sleep well. There are blue light cancelling softwares and apps available. If you absolutely must be using your gadget until before sleep, use these apps.

13. Avoid smoking: Smoking is associated with a wide range of illnesses and disorders. Smoking also throws your sleep pattern out of gear. While physiologically, if you are addicted to nicotine, you may feel that smoking helps you sleep, it isn't true.

14. Exercise: If the body burns calories and becomes physically tired, the tiredness will allow better sleep. Working out increases the heart rate and that improves sleep. It also helps to release extra energy and calms the body down, which can lead to improved sleep.

15. Get sunlight: Being out in the sunlight reinforces the correct circadian rhythm, which as mentioned also works on the light and darkness. Exposure to sunlight creates a distinct differentiation between light and darkness. In addition, exposure to sunlight releases serotonin which allows better focus. And when you move from the sun to the dark, the body releases melatonin which helps in better sleep.

16. Free your mind: Ruminating over events that went wrong in the day will affect your sleep. Turn to relaxation exercises like mindful breathing, grounding, and progressive muscle relaxation to cast of your worries for the evening. You can always pick them back up the following morning. But if you want to sleep well, free your mind every evening.

17. Wake up at the same time: No matter how much or how little you sleep, make sure that you get out of bed at the same time every morning. Getting out of bed means not using the snooze button, and jumping out of bed, no matter how late you have slept. When the body is allowed to learn the time allocated for sleep, better sleep follows.

18. Avoid long naps in the afternoon: If you have been unable to sleep well in the night, you may take a power nap, but the power nap should not exceed 30 minutes. Any more than that and will disrupt the sleeping pattern again, and make it difficult for you to sleep at night.

19. Don't force yourself: If you realize that even after 20 minutes of trying to sleep, that you are still not sleepy, get out of bed. There is no point in tossing and turning in bed and not being able to sleep. Engage in some light activity like reading a book for some time.

20. Avoid sleeping in on weekends: If we have worked hard during the week, we believe that if we wake up later in the morning on weekends, it is sufficient to cover up for the lost sleep. But that is not true. You must avoid doing that and for that you should try to get sufficient sleep on weekdays.

21. Do not try to average out: Like the previous point, it is no good trying to average out sleep. You cannot say *'I have to sleep 56 hours in 7 days so I will sleep for 4 hours per day on weekdays and 18 hours per day on weekends'*. It doesn't work that way either.

22. Beds are for sleep and sex only: The bed should be used for only two reasons. Sleep and sex. If what you are doing is neither of these two get up and do whatever you are doing sitting up. So, avoid watching TV in bed, reading in bed or eating in bed.

23. Change your schedule gradually: After reading all this and other tips that you come across, if you intend to change your schedule, do so gradually. Do not jump right into changing your schedule at once. Allow your body to get used to the changed pattern. Give it time.

If you follow these tips regularly, you should notice an improvement in sleep. If despite doing all this regularly, you are still not able to sleep, you should consult a doctor to rule out a sleeping disorder.

Additional Resource 4: The Poem
The Blind Men and the Elephant - J. G. Saxe

It was six men of Indostan
To learning much inclined,
Who went to see the Elephant
(Though all of them were blind),
That each by observation
Might satisfy his mind.

The First approached the Elephant,
And happening to fall
Against his broad and sturdy side,
At once began to bawl:
'God bless me! but the Elephant
Is very like a WALL!'

The Second, feeling of the tusk,
Cried, 'Ho, what have we here,
So very round and smooth and sharp?
To me 'tis mighty clear
This wonder of an Elephant
Is very like a SPEAR!'

The Third approached the animal,
And happening to take
The squirming trunk within his hands,
Thus boldly up and spake:
'I see,' quoth he, 'the Elephant
Is very like a SNAKE!'

The Fourth reached out an eager hand,
And felt about the knee
'What most this wondrous beast is like
Is mighty plain,' quoth he:
''Tis clear enough the Elephant
Is very like a TREE!'

The Fifth, who chanced to touch the ear,
Said: 'E'en the blindest man
Can tell what this resembles most;
Deny the fact who can,
This marvel of an Elephant
Is very like a FAN!'

The Sixth no sooner had begun
About the beast to grope,
Than seizing on the swinging tail
That fell within his scope,
'I see,' quoth he, 'the Elephant
Is very like a ROPE!'

And so these men of Indostan
Disputed loud and long,
Each in his own opinion
Exceeding stiff and strong,
Though each was partly in the right,
And all were in the wrong!

So, oft in theologic wars,
The disputants, I ween,
Tread on in utter ignorance,
Of what each other mean,
And prate about the elephant,
Not one of them has seen!

Additional Resource 5: Y-BOCS Symptom Checklist - Obsessions

Type	Obsessions	Examples
Aggression	I fear I might harm myself	Fear of eating with a knife or fork
Aggression	I fear I might harm myself	Fear of handling sharp objects
Aggression	I fear I might harm myself	Fear of walking near glass windows
Aggression	I fear I might harm other people	Fear of poisoning other people's food
Aggression	I fear I might harm other people	Fear of harming babies
Aggression	I fear I might harm other people	Fear of pushing someone in front of a train
Aggression	I fear I might harm other people	Fear of hurting someone's feelings
Aggression	I fear I might harm other people	Fear of being responsible by not providing assistance for some imagined catastrophe
Aggression	I fear I might harm other people	Fear of causing harm by giving bad advice.
Aggression	I have violent or horrific images in my mind	Images of murder
Aggression	I have violent or horrific images in my mind	Images of dismembered bodies
Aggression	I have violent or horrific images in my mind	Images of other disgusting scenes
Aggression	I fear I will blurt out obscenities	Fear of shouting obscenities in public situations like church, temple
Aggression	I fear I will blurt out obscenities	Fear of shouting obscenities in public places like cinema theatres, malls
Aggression	I fear I will blurt out obscenities	Fear of writing obscenities
Aggression	I fear doing something embarrassing	Fear of appearing foolish in social situations
Aggression	I fear I will act on an unwanted impulse	Fear of driving a car into a tree
Aggression	I fear I will act on an unwanted impulse	Fear of running someone over

Aggression	I fear I will act on an unwanted impulse	Fear of stabbing a friend
Aggression	I fear I will steal things	Fear of 'cheating' a cashier
Aggression	I fear I will steal things	Fear of shoplifting inexpensive items
Aggression	I fear that I'll harm others because I'm not careful enough	Fear of causing an accident without being aware of it (such as a hit-and-run accident)
Aggression	I fear I'll be responsible for something else terrible happening.	Fear of causing a fire or burglary because of not being careful enough in checking the house before leaving
Contamination	I am concerned or disgusted with bodily waste or secretions	Fear of contracting AIDS, cancer, or other diseases from public rest rooms
Contamination	I am concerned or disgusted with bodily waste or secretions	Fear of your own saliva, urine, feces, semen, or vaginal secretions
Contamination	I am concerned with dirt or germs	Fear of picking up germs from sitting in certain chairs
Contamination	I am concerned with dirt or germs	Fear of picking up germs from shaking hands
Contamination	I am concerned with dirt or germs	Fear of picking up germs from touching door handles
Contamination	I am excessively concerned with environmental contaminants	Fear of being contaminated by asbestos or radon
Contamination	I am excessively concerned with environmental contaminants	Fear of radioactive substances
Contamination	I am excessively concerned with environmental contaminants	Fear of things associated with towns containing toxic waste sights
Contamination	I am excessively concerned with certain household cleansers	Fear of poisonous kitchen or bathroom cleansers
Contamination	I am excessively concerned with certain household cleansers	Fear of poisonous solvents
Contamination	I am excessively concerned with certain household cleansers	Fear of poisonous insect spray
Contamination	I am excessively concerned with certain household cleansers	Fear of poisonous turpentine

Contamination	I am excessively concerned with animals	Fear of being contaminated by touching an insect, dog, cat, or other animal
Contamination	I am bothered by sticky substances or residues	Fear of adhesive tape or other sticky substances that may trap contaminants
Contamination	I am concerned that I will get ill because of contamination	Fear of getting ill as a direct result of being contaminated
Contamination	I am concerned that I will contaminate others	Fear of touching other people after you touch poisonous substances (like gasoline) or after you touch your own body
Contamination	I am concerned that I will contaminate others	Fear of preparing food after you touch poisonous substances (like gasoline) or after you touch your own body
Sexual	I have forbidden or perverse sexual thoughts, images, or impulses	Unwanted sexual thoughts about strangers, family, or friends
Sexual	I have sexual obsessions that involve children or incest	Unwanted thoughts about sexually molesting either your own children or other children
Sexual	I have obsessions about homosexuality	Worries like 'Am I a homosexual?' or 'What if I suddenly become gay?'
Sexual	I have obsessions about aggressive sexual behavior toward other people	Unwanted images of violent sexual behavior toward adult strangers, friends, or family members
Hoarding	I have obsessions about hoarding or saving things	Worries about throwing away seemingly unimportant things that you might need in the future
Hoarding	I have obsessions about hoarding or saving things	Urges to pick up and collect useless things
Religious	I am concerned with sacrilege and blasphemy	Worries about having blasphemous thoughts
Religious	I am concerned with sacrilege and blasphemy	Worries about saying blasphemous things
Religious	I am concerned with sacrilege and blasphemy	Worries about being punished for blasphemy
Religious	I am excessively concerned with morality	Worries about always doing 'the right thing,'
Religious	I am excessively concerned with morality	Worries about having told a lie

Religious	I am excessively concerned with morality	Worries about having cheated someone
Need for Symmetry or Exactness	I have obsessions about symmetry or exactness	Worries about papers and books being properly aligned
Need for Symmetry or Exactness	I have obsessions about symmetry or exactness	Worries about calculations being perfect
Need for Symmetry or Exactness	I have obsessions about symmetry or exactness	Worries about handwriting being perfect
Miscellaneous	I feel that I need to know or remember certain things	Belief that you need to remember license plate numbers
Miscellaneous	I feel that I need to know or remember certain things	Belief that you need to remember the names of actors on television shows
Miscellaneous	I feel that I need to know or remember certain things	Belief that you need to remember old telephone numbers
Miscellaneous	I feel that I need to know or remember certain things	Belief that you need to remember bumper stickers
Miscellaneous	I feel that I need to know or remember certain things	Belief that you need to remember t-shirt slogans
Miscellaneous	I fear saying certain things	Fear of saying certain words (such as 'thirteen') because of superstitions
Miscellaneous	I fear saying certain things	Fear of saying something that might be disrespectful to a dead person
Miscellaneous	I fear saying certain things	Fear of using words with an apostrophe (because this denotes possession)
Miscellaneous	I fear not saying just the right thing	Fear of having said the wrong thing
Miscellaneous	I fear not saying just the right thing	Fear of not using the 'perfect' word
Miscellaneous	I fear losing things	Worries about losing a wallet or other unimportant objects, like a scrap of note paper
Miscellaneous	I am bothered by intrusive (neutral) mental images	Random, unwanted images in your mind

Miscellaneous	I am bothered by intrusive mental nonsense sounds, words or music	Words, songs, or music in your mind that you can't stop
Miscellaneous	I am bothered by certain sounds or noises	Worries about the sounds of clocks ticking loudly or voices in another room that may interfere with sleeping
Miscellaneous	I have lucky and unlucky numbers	Worries about common numbers (like thirteen) that may cause you to perform activities a certain number of times
Miscellaneous	I have lucky and unlucky numbers	Worries about common numbers (like thirteen) that may cause you to postpone an action until a certain lucky hour of the day
Miscellaneous	Certain colors have special significance to me	Fear of using objects of certain colors (e.g. black may be associated with death, red with blood or injury)
Miscellaneous	I have superstitious fears	Fear of passing a cemetery, hearse, or black cat
Miscellaneous	I have superstitious fears	Fear of omens associated with death
Somatic	I am concerned with illness or disease	Worries that you have an illness like cancer, heart disease or AIDS, despite reassurance from doctors that you do not
Somatic	I am excessively concerned with a part of my body or an aspect of my appearance (dysmorphophobia)	Worries that your face, ears, nose, eyes, or another part of your body is hideous, ugly, despite reassurances to the contrary

Additional Resource 6: Y-BOCS Symptom Checklist - Compulsions

Type	Compulsion	Examples
Contamination	I wash my hands excessively or in a ritualized way	Washing your hands many times a day or for long periods of time after touching, or thinking that you have touched a contaminated object. This may include washing the entire length of your arms
Contamination	I have excessive or ritualized showering, bathing, tooth brushing, grooming, or toilet routines	Taking showers or baths or performing other bathroom routines that may last for several hours. If the sequence is interrupted, the entire process may have to be restarted
Contamination	I have compulsions that involve cleaning household items or other inanimate objects	Excessive cleaning of faucets, toilets, floors, kitchen counters, or kitchen utensils
Contamination	I do other things to prevent or remove contact with contaminants	Asking family members to handle or remove insecticides, garbage, gasoline cans, raw meat, paints, varnish, drugs in the medicine cabinet.
Contamination		If you can't avoid these things, you may wear gloves or use paper napkins to handle them.
Checking	I check that I did not harm others	Checking that you haven't hurt someone without knowing it. You may ask others for reassurance or telephone to make sure that everything is all right
Checking	I check that I did not harm myself	Looking for injuries of bleeding after handling sharp or breakable objects. You may frequently go to doctors to ask for reassurance that you haven't hurt yourself
Checking	I check that nothing terrible happened	Searching for news about some catastrophe that you believe you caused. You may also ask people for reassurance that you didn't cause an accident.

193

Checking	I check that I did not make a mistake	Repeated checking of door locks, stoves, electrical outlets, before leaving home; repeated checking while reading, writing, or doing simple calculations to make sure that you didn't make a mistake
Checking	I check some aspect of my physical condition tied to my obsessions about my body	Seeking reassurance from friends or doctors that you aren't having a heart attack or getting cancer
Checking		Repeatedly taking pulse, blood pressure, or temperature
Checking		Checking your appearance in a mirror, looking for ugly features
Repetition	I reread or rewrite things	Taking hours to read a few pages in a book or to write a short letter because you get caught in a cycle of reading and rereading
Repetition		Worrying that you didn't understand something you just read
Repetition		Searching for a 'perfect' word or phrase
Repetition		Having obsessive thoughts about the shape of certain printed letters in a book
Repetition	I need to repeat routine activities	Repeating activities like turning appliances on and off
Repetition		Repeating activities like combing your hair
Repetition		Repeating activities like going in and out of a doorway
Repetition		Repeating activities like looking in a particular direction not feeling comfortable unless you do these things the 'right' number of times
Counting	I have counting compulsions	Counting objects like ceiling or floor tiles
Counting		Counting objects like books in a bookcase
Counting		Counting objects like grains of sand on a beach

Counting		Counting when you repeat certain activities, like washing
Ordering/Arrangement	I have ordering or arranging compulsions	Wasting hours arranging things in your house in 'order' and then becoming very upset if this order is disturbed
Ordering/Arrangement		Straightening paper and pens on a desktop or books in a bookcase
Hoarding	I have compulsions to hoard or collect things	Saving old newspapers, notes, cans, paper towels, wrappers and empty bottles for fear that if you throw them away you may need them
Hoarding		Picking up useless objects from the street or from garbage cans
Miscellaneous	I have mental rituals (other than checking/counting)	Performing rituals in your head, like saying prayers or thinking a 'good' thought to undo a 'bad' thought.
Miscellaneous	I need to tell, ask, or confess	Asking other people to reassure you, confessing to wrong behaviors you never even did, believing that you have to tell other people certain words to feel better
Miscellaneous	I need to touch, tap, or rub things	Giving in to the urge to touch rough surfaces, like wood, or hot surfaces, like a stove top
Miscellaneous		Giving in to the urge to lightly touch other people
Miscellaneous		Believing you need to touch an object like a telephone to prevent an illness in your family
Miscellaneous	I take measures (other than checking) to prevent harm or terrible consequences to myself or family	Staying away from sharp or breakable objects, such as knives, scissors, and fragile glass
Miscellaneous	I have ritualized eating behaviors	Arranging your food, knife, and fork in a particular order before being able to eat
Miscellaneous		Eating according to a strict ritual
Miscellaneous		Not being able to eat until the hands of a clock point exactly at a certain time

Miscellaneous	I have superstitious behaviors	Not taking a bus or train if its number contains an 'unlucky' number (like thirteen)
Miscellaneous		Staying in your house on the thirteenth of the month
Miscellaneous		Throwing away clothes you wore while passing a funeral home or cemetery
Miscellaneous	I pull my hair out (trichotillomania)	Pulling hair from your scalp, eyelids, eyelashes, or pubic areas, using your fingers or tweezers. You may produce bald spots, or you may pluck your eyebrows or eyelids smooth

Additional Resource 7: Rationalization of Compulsions

A		Monitoring your own feelings and sensations
1	Rationalization (Non Triggered State)	Why do I need to monitor my feelings? - To check if I feel good about my partner. Why do I need to feel good? - To know if I am with the right partner. Would I leave my partner under any circumstances? - No. So, is the answer really important? - No. So, is monitoring helpful? - No.
2	Mindful Acceptance of ROCD (Triggered State)	I have ROCD. These thoughts are my ROCD thoughts. I am okay with getting these obsessive thoughts. These thoughts also seem real, which is okay too.
3	Distancing from the Obsession (Triggered State)	This is Kay's deviousness. Kay is asking me to give meaning to the obsession that I may not be with the right partner. Kay always lies to me and is only interested in making my life miserable.
4	Distancing from the Compulsion (Triggered State)	I am being given the urge to monitor my feelings and sensations by Kay and I will not do the compulsion.
5	Response Prevention (Triggered State)	If I do not monitor and things go wrong, that is, I realize later that I was with the wrong partner, I will handle it then. I will not dwell on it now

B		Researching and checking
1	Rationalization (Non Triggered State)	Why do I need to research? - To know if what is happening to me is common or unique. Why do I need to know that? - So that it provides me relief to know that I am not alone. Does knowing that I am not alone make this go away or do I need to keep doing it all the time? - I do it all the time. So, is it helpful? - No.
2	Mindful Acceptance of ROCD (Triggered State)	I have ROCD. These thoughts are my ROCD thoughts. I am okay with getting these obsessive thoughts. These thoughts also seem real, which is okay too.
3	Distancing from the Obsession (Triggered State)	This is Kay's deviousness. Kay is asking me to give meaning to the obsession that I don't want to be alone in this. Kay always lies to me and is only interested in making my life miserable.
4	Distancing from the Compulsion (Triggered State)	I am being given the urge to research and check by Kay and I will not do the compulsion.
5	Response Prevention (Triggered State)	If I do not research and check and things go wrong, that is, I realize later that the problem with my partner was unique and I could have escaped it, I will handle it then. I will not dwell on it now

197

C		Comparison
1	**Rationalization (Non Triggered State)**	Why do I need to compare? - To make sure that my partner is the best. Why should my partner be the best? - So that I do not feel like I am compromising in the relationship. Why do I not want to compromise in the relationship? - Because I want my brother to approve of my choice. If my brother does not approve of my choice, would I leave my partner in favor of someone else who seems better? - No. Does comparing help then? - No
2	**Mindful Acceptance of ROCD (Triggered State)**	I have ROCD. These thoughts are my ROCD thoughts. I am okay with getting these obsessive thoughts. These thoughts also seem real, which is okay too.
3	**Distancing from the Obsession (Triggered State)**	This is Kay's deviousness. Kay is asking me to give meaning to the obsession that my partner may not be the best. Kay always lies to me and is only interested in making my life miserable.
4	**Distancing from the Compulsion (Triggered State)**	I am being given the urge to compare by Kay and I will not do the compulsion.
5	**Response Prevention (Triggered State)**	If I do not compare and things go wrong, that is, I realize later that my brother does not approve of my choice, I will handle it then. I will not dwell on it now

D		Reassurance seeking
1	**Rationalization (Non Triggered State)**	Why do I need to seek reassurance? - To confirm what I am thinking is true. Why do I need to confirm that? - So that I do not make a mistake. Why must I not make a mistake? - So that I am 100% sure that I am in the right relationship. If I am not reassured about being in the right relationship, will I leave my partner? - No. So, is reassurance seeking helpful? - No
2	**Mindful Acceptance of ROCD (Triggered State)**	I have ROCD. These thoughts are my ROCD thoughts. I am okay with getting these obsessive thoughts. These thoughts also seem real, which is okay too.
3	**Distancing from the Obsession (Triggered State)**	This is Kay's deviousness. Kay is asking me to give meaning to the obsession that I may not be doing the right thing. Kay always lies to me and is only interested in making my life miserable.
4	**Distancing from the Compulsion (Triggered State)**	I am being given the urge to seek reassurance by Kay and I will not do the compulsion.
5	**Response Prevention (Triggered State)**	If I do not seek reassurance and things go wrong, that is, I realize later that I was not 100% sure about being in the right relationship, I will handle it then. I will not dwell on it now

E		Neutralizing your thoughts
1	**Rationalization (Non Triggered State)**	Why do I need to neutralize my thoughts? - Because I don't want my thoughts to be true. Why do I not want my thoughts to be true? - As proof that I have not made a mistake. Does neutralizing help in providing that proof? - No. If I am not convinced about the correctness of my decision, will I leave my partner? - No. So, is neutralizing helpful? - No
2	**Mindful Acceptance of ROCD (Triggered State)**	I have ROCD. These thoughts are my ROCD thoughts. I am okay with getting these obsessive thoughts. These thoughts also seem real, which is okay too.
3	**Distancing from the Obsession (Triggered State)**	This is Kay's deviousness. Kay is asking me to give meaning to the obsession that I may not be with the right partner. Kay always lies to me and is only interested in making my life miserable.
4	**Distancing from the Compulsion (Triggered State)**	I am being given the urge to neutralize my thoughts by Kay and I will not do the compulsion.
5	**Response Prevention (Triggered State)**	If I do not neutralize my thoughts and things go wrong, that is, I realize later that I did make a mistake by being in the relationship, I will handle it then. I will not dwell on it now

F		Post-facto rumination
1	**Rationalization (Non Triggered State)**	Why do I need to ruminate after an event? - To see whether my partner reacted appropriately . Why is it important for my partner to react appropriately? - So that people do not look down upon me for being in the wrong relationship. If people look down upon me for being in the wrong relationship, would I leave my partner? No. So, does it help to engage in post-facto rumination? - No.
2	**Mindful Acceptance of ROCD (Triggered State)**	I have ROCD. These thoughts are my ROCD thoughts. I am okay with getting these obsessive thoughts. These thoughts also seem real, which is okay too.
3	**Distancing from the Obsession (Triggered State)**	This is Kay's deviousness. Kay is asking me to give meaning to the obsession that my partner did not behave appropriately. Kay always lies to me and is only interested in making my life miserable.
4	**Distancing from the Compulsion (Triggered State)**	I am being given the urge to engage in post-facto rumination by Kay and I will not do the compulsion.
5	**Response Prevention (Triggered State)**	If I do not ruminate post-facto and things go wrong, that is, I realize later that people looked down upon me for being with someone who does not behave appropriately, I will handle it then. I will not dwell on it now

G		Attempt to change your partner
1	Rationalization (Non Triggered State)	Why do I need to change my partner? - So that my partner fits in . Does my partner respond to such attempts well? - No. Even if my partner makes changes, am I happy? - No. If my partner does not make changes, am I considering leaving my partner? - No. Then are these attempts helpful? - No
2	Mindful Acceptance of ROCD (Triggered State)	I have ROCD. These thoughts are my ROCD thoughts. I am okay with getting these obsessive thoughts. These thoughts also seem real, which is okay too.
3	Distancing from the Obsession (Triggered State)	This is Kay's deviousness. Kay is asking me to give meaning to the obsession that my partner needs to make changes to fit in. Kay always lies to me and is only interested in making my life miserable.
4	Distancing from the Compulsion (Triggered State)	I am being given the urge to force my partner to change by Kay and I will not do the compulsion.
5	Response Prevention (Triggered State)	If I do not attempt to change my partner and things go wrong, that is, I realize later that my partner does not fit in, I will handle it then. I will not dwell on it now

H		Avoidance
1	Rationalization (Non Triggered State)	Why do I need to avoid? - Because if I face my triggers it causes me anxiety. Does avoiding make the fear go away or just suppresses it? - Just suppresses it. If I accidentally come across a trigger that I have been avoiding, is my anxiety less or more? - More. So, will avoidance help me manage my anxiety in the long run? - No.
2	Mindful Acceptance of ROCD (Triggered State)	I have ROCD. These thoughts are my ROCD thoughts. I am okay with getting these obsessive thoughts. These thoughts also seem real, which is okay too.
3	Distancing from the Obsession (Triggered State)	This is Kay's deviousness. Kay is telling me to avoid anxiety. Kay always lies to me and is only interested in making my life miserable.
4	Distancing from the Compulsion (Triggered State)	I am being given the urge to avoid by Kay and I will not do the compulsion.
5	Response Prevention (Triggered State)	If I do not engage in avoidance and things go wrong, that is, I get triggered and am not able to handle my anxiety, I will handle it then. I will not dwell on it now

I		Proxy compulsion
1	**Rationalization (Non Triggered State)**	Why do I need to engage in proxy compulsion? - Because if I do it myself, I will be more anxious. Does that amount to avoidance? - Yes. Is avoidance good? - No. So, is proxy compulsion helpful? - No.
2	**Mindful Acceptance of ROCD (Triggered State)**	I have ROCD. These thoughts are my ROCD thoughts. I am okay with getting these obsessive thoughts. These thoughts also seem real, which is okay too.
3	**Distancing from the Obsession (Triggered State)**	This is Kay's deviousness. Kay is asking me to give meaning to the obsession that I cannot do things on my own. Kay always lies to me and is only interested in making my life miserable.
4	**Distancing from the Compulsion (Triggered State)**	I am being given the urge to engage in proxy compulsion by Kay and I will not do the compulsion.
5	**Response Prevention (Triggered State)**	If I do not engage in proxy compulsion and things go wrong, that is, I realize later that I am terribly anxious for doing things myself, I will handle it then. I will not dwell on it now

J		Negative self-talk (NST)
1	**Rationalization (Non Triggered State)**	Why do I engage in NST? Because I feel I make a lot of mistakes. Why do I feel I cannot make mistakes? - Because it would make me imperfect. What would being imperfect mean? - I would have low self worth. Does NST help in make me feel worthy? - No. So, does NST help? - No
2	**Mindful Acceptance of ROCD (Triggered State)**	I have ROCD. These thoughts are my ROCD thoughts. I am okay with getting these obsessive thoughts. These thoughts also seem real, which is okay too.
3	**Distancing from the Obsession (Triggered State)**	This is Kay's deviousness. Kay is asking me to give meaning to the obsession that I make more mistakes than anyone else. Kay always lies to me and is only interested in making my life miserable.
4	**Distancing from the Compulsion (Triggered State)**	I am being given the urge to engage in NST by Kay and I will not do the compulsion.
5	**Response Prevention (Triggered State)**	If I do not engage in NST and things go wrong, that is, I realize later that I have indeed made more mistakes than other people, I will handle it then. I will not dwell on it now

K		Distraction
1	**Rationalization (Non Triggered State)**	Why do I need to distract my mind? - Because the obsessive thoughts cause me a lot of anxiety. Does that amount to an attempt at avoidance of thought? Yes. Is avoidance good? - No. So, is distraction going to help? - No.
2	**Mindful Acceptance of ROCD (Triggered State)**	I have ROCD. These thoughts are my ROCD thoughts. I am okay with getting these obsessive thoughts. These thoughts also seem real, which is okay too.
3	**Distancing from the Obsession (Triggered State)**	This is Kay's deviousness. Kay is telling me that I cannot handle the anxiety on my own. Kay always lies to me and is only interested in making my life miserable.
4	**Distancing from the Compulsion (Triggered State)**	I am being given the urge to distract myself by Kay and I will not do the compulsion.
5	**Response Prevention (Triggered State)**	If I do not distract myself and things go wrong, that is, I am massively triggered and anxious, I will handle it then. I will not dwell on it now

L		Confession
1	**Rationalization (Non Triggered State)**	Why do I need to confess to my partner? - Because I think I am being unfaithful otherwise. Does my partner appreciate my confessions? - No, we end up fighting more. Is it helping the relationship or worsening it? - Worsening it. So, is confessing helpful? - No.
2	**Mindful Acceptance of ROCD (Triggered State)**	I have ROCD. These thoughts are my ROCD thoughts. I am okay with getting these obsessive thoughts. These thoughts also seem real, which is okay too.
3	**Distancing from the Obsession (Triggered State)**	This is Kay's deviousness. Kay is asking me to give meaning to the obsession that I am unfaithful. Kay always lies to me and is only interested in making my life miserable.
4	**Distancing from the Compulsion (Triggered State)**	I am being given the urge to confess by Kay and I will not do the compulsion.
5	**Response Prevention (Triggered State)**	If I do not confess and things go wrong, that is, I realize later that I was being unfaithful, I will handle it then. I will not dwell on it now

M		Stalking social media
1	**Rationalization (Non Triggered State)**	Why do I need to stalk my partner's social media accounts? - To find evidence that my partner does not love me. What evidence? - That my partner seems happy without us being in them together. Is that correct? - No but my mind tells me so. Should I believe what Kay tells then? - I should go with what I know. Is stalking social media helpful then? - No
2	**Mindful Acceptance of ROCD (Triggered State)**	I have ROCD. These thoughts are my ROCD thoughts. I am okay with getting these obsessive thoughts. These thoughts also seem real, which is okay too.
3	**Distancing from the Obsession (Triggered State)**	This is Kay's deviousness. Kay is asking me to give meaning to the obsession that my partner is unhappy with me. Kay always lies to me and is only interested in making my life miserable.
4	**Distancing from the Compulsion (Triggered State)**	I am being given the urge to stalk my partner's social media by Kay and I will not do the compulsion.
5	**Response Prevention (Triggered State)**	If I do not stalk my partner's social media and things go wrong, that is, I realize later that my partner was being unfaithful, I will handle it then. I will not dwell on it now

N		Lashing out at partner
1	**Rationalization (Non Triggered State)**	Why do I need to lash out at my partner? - Because I think my partner should respond to my texts immediately and the way I want her to. What does it mean to me if she doesn't? - It probably means she is with someone else and happy without me. Is that the only explanation? - No but my mind says so. Should I believe what Kay tells me then? - I should go with what I know. Is lashing out at my partner working well for our relationship? - No, it isn't
2	**Mindful Acceptance of ROCD (Triggered State)**	I have ROCD. These thoughts are my ROCD thoughts. I am okay with getting these obsessive thoughts. These thoughts also seem real, which is okay too.
3	**Distancing from the Obsession (Triggered State)**	This is Kay's deviousness. Kay is asking me to give meaning to the obsession that my partner is happy with someone else. Kay always lies to me and is only interested in making my life miserable.
4	**Distancing from the Compulsion (Triggered State)**	I am being given the urge to lash out at my partner by Kay and I will not do the compulsion.
5	**Response Prevention (Triggered State)**	If I do not lash out to keep my partner in check and things go wrong, that is, I realize later that she was indeed happier with someone else, I will handle it then. I will not dwell on it now

203

O		Apologizing excessively
1	**Rationalization (Non Triggered State)**	Why do I need to apologize? - Because I think I may have made a mistake and it will offend the other person. Why should my partner not be offended? - Because I do not want her to break ties with me. Would I break ties with her if the situation was reversed? - No. Do I have any indication that my partner intends to break ties with me if I do not apologize? - No. Does apologizing excessively help then? - No.
2	**Mindful Acceptance of ROCD (Triggered State)**	I have ROCD. These thoughts are my ROCD thoughts. I am okay with getting these obsessive thoughts. These thoughts also seem real, which is okay too.
3	**Distancing from the Obsession (Triggered State)**	This is Kay's deviousness. Kay is asking me to give meaning to the obsession that my partner may take offense if I do not apologize. Kay always lies to me and is only interested in making my life miserable.
4	**Distancing from the Compulsion (Triggered State)**	I am being given the urge to apologize to my partner by Kay and I will not do the compulsion.
5	**Response Prevention (Triggered State)**	If I do not apologize excessively and things go wrong, that is, I realize later that my partner did take offense, I will handle it then. I will not dwell on it now

P		Pre-planning
1	**Rationalization (Non Triggered State)**	Why do I need to pre-plan? - Because I may not be able to handle the triggering situation. Why do I need to handle the triggering situation? - So that I can minimize the anxiety. Is minimizing anxiety artificially the right thing to do? - No it isn't. So, should I be trying to minimize the anxiety artificially? - No. Does that mean that pre-planning is helpful? - No.
2	**Mindful Acceptance of ROCD (Triggered State)**	I have ROCD. These thoughts are my ROCD thoughts. I am okay with getting these obsessive thoughts. These thoughts also seem real, which is okay too.
3	**Distancing from the Obsession (Triggered State)**	This is Kay's deviousness. Kay is asking me to give meaning to the obsession that I may not be able to handle the anxiety. Kay always lies to me and is only interested in making my life miserable.
4	**Distancing from the Compulsion (Triggered State)**	I am being given the urge to pre-plan for a situation by Kay and I will not do the compulsion.
5	**Response Prevention (Triggered State)**	If I do not seek reassurance and things go wrong, that is, I realize later that I was not able to handle the anxiety, I will handle it then. I will not dwell on it now

Q		Monitoring partner's feelings and behavior
1	**Rationalization (Non Triggered State)**	Why do I need to monitor my partner's feelings and behavior? - Because I may be upsetting my partner when I am triggered. Why don't I want to upset my partner? - So that my partner does not leave me. Would I break ties with my partner if she was triggered and apprehensive about breaking ties with me? - No. Does that mean that the monitoring my partner's feelings and behavior is needed? - No.
2	**Mindful Acceptance of ROCD (Triggered State)**	I have ROCD. These thoughts are my ROCD thoughts. I am okay with getting these obsessive thoughts. These thoughts also seem real, which is okay too.
3	**Distancing from the Obsession (Triggered State)**	This is Kay's deviousness. Kay is asking me to give meaning to the obsession that my partner may leave me if she sees me so triggered. Kay always lies to me and is only interested in making my life miserable.
4	**Distancing from the Compulsion (Triggered State)**	I am being given the urge to monitor my partner's feelings and behavior by Kay and I will not do the compulsion.
5	**Response Prevention (Triggered State)**	If I do not monitor my partner's feelings and behavior and things go wrong, that is, I realize later that my partner does leave me seeing me so triggered, I will handle it then. I will not dwell on it now

Additional Resource 8: Imaginal Script Examples

Example 1: For the avoidance compulsion

I have been in therapy and I have been asked not to avoid meeting people I find attractive. I am at a party and I see a good looking girl who seems to be attracted to me as well. I decide to not avoid her and go up to talk to her. I find her very hot and she seems to be sexually drawn to me too.

We get out of the party and go to her place where we have hot, torrid sex, which I love. I have cheated on my girlfriend and she gets to know. She slaps me and decides to dump me. She goes away with an ex-boyfriend and I am shattered.

My friends come to know and they are on my girlfriend's side too. They criticize me and abandon me as well. My family also looks at me contemptuously and breaks ties with me. The girl from the party I slept with does not want to have a relationship with me. I am all alone. I keep cursing myself for not having avoided going up to the girl but there is no point anymore.

Additional pointers to make the script more severe

- The girl from the party is a minor and I am arrested for pedophilia.
- The girl from the party gives me a sexually transmitted disease and ruins my life.
- My girlfriend is happy and I end up committing suicide.

Possible Escape Hatches to be aware of

- My girlfriend forgives my mistake.
- My friends introduce me to another girl.
- The girl from the party becomes my new girlfriend.

Example 2: For the Stalking Social Media compulsion

I have been in therapy for my ROCD and my therapist has asked me to stop stalking my partner's social media feeds for possible infidelity. My girlfriend has told me that she would not be able to meet me today because she has work at office.

Normally I would stalk her social media to see if she is posting anything but I decide not to. It turns out that she did not have work at office but she was going to a party with another date. She has finally decided that she has had enough of me and decided to cheat on me.

I find out through a friend who has seen her social media posts. When I ask her about it, she is remorseless and laughs at me instead. Her new boyfriend also laughs at me and they mock me for crying. I had wanted to settle down with her but she clearly was not happy with me.

My friends also criticize me for not having checked social media to keep tabs on my cheating girlfriend. I am all alone and wish I had been a little more vigilant about keeping tabs on my girlfriend.

Additional pointers to make the script more severe

- My girlfriend has been cheating on me for a long time.
- The boy she is cheating on me with is my best friend or brother.
- My girlfriend is happy with her new boyfriend and I end up committing suicide.

Possible Escape Hatches to be aware of

- My girlfriend turns out to be innocent.
- My friends introduce me to another girl who is better.
- My girlfriend realizes her mistake and comes back to me.

Worksheets

Worksheet 1 - Obsessions or Compulsions

For each of the following statements, write O if it is an obsession and C if it is a compulsion.

No	Statement	Response
1	Neutralizing a bad thought by replacing it with a good thought	
2	Horrific images in the mind	
3	Thoughts of losing or not having things you might need.	
4	Confessing excessively	
5	Intrusive sexually explicit or violent thoughts and image	
6	Rereading or rewriting something repeatedly	
7	Ordering or arranging things to get them just right	
8	Excessive toilet routines	
9	Fear of being a paedophile	
10	Checking in on loved ones to make sure they're safe.	
11	Thoughts of being contaminated	
12	Thoughts of loss of control and harming yourself or others.	
13	Accumulating "junk" such as old newspapers or bags.	
14	Counting without being able to stop	
15	Walking in and out of rooms repeatedly	
16	Thoughts of being homosexual	
17	Checking repeatedly for mistakes	
18	Fear of being becoming dirty or making others dirty.	
19	Fear of stealing things.	
20	Superstitions; excessive attention to good luck and bad luck concepts	
21	Excessive focus on religious or moral ideas.	
22	Counting, tapping, repeating certain words.	
23	Urge to strip in public	
24	Sexually inappropriate images in the mind	
25	Excessive double-checking of locks, appliances, and switches.	
26	Repeating something a 'safe' number of times	
27	Avoidance of contaminants	
28	Urge to shout expletives in public	

No	Statement	Response
29	Order and symmetry: the idea that everything must line up properly.	
30	Need for evenness and perfection	
31	Fear of committing sin	
32	Thoughts of being sick	
33	Reviewing events to prevent harm	
34	Concern about right and wrong	
35	Praying excessively or engaging in rituals triggered by religious fear.	
36	Spending a lot of time washing or cleaning	
37	Need for having the perfect memory	
38	Controlling hand movements to not harm someone	
39	Asking someone repeatedly to confirm something	
40	Fear of accidentally or purposefully running over someone	

Answers to Worksheet 1 - Obsessions or Compulsions

1. **Compulsion.** Neutralizing is a common compulsion in OCD, in which a person tries to push out a bad thought out of the mind. The bad thought is the obsession.

2. **Obsession.** Automatic images in the brain, which cause distress, and over which you have no control are an obsession. Trying to get rid of them is the compulsion.

3. **Obsession.** Fear of inadequacy is an obsession, which you want to prevent. Excessive preparation to prevent this from coming true is the compulsion.

4. **Compulsion.** Confessions are used as a compulsion to relieve the anxiety of holding something in and feeling you are bad because of that. The feeling of wrongdoing is the obsession.

5. **Obsession.** Sexually intrusive thoughts are distressing and you want to shut them down. So, they are obsessions. The act of trying to shut them down is the compulsion.

6. **Compulsion.** Repeating an activity is a compulsion to try to reduce the anxiety associated with not having done something well. The feeling of not doing well is the obsession.

7. **Compulsion.** Ordering and arranging something is a compulsion to reduce the anxiety from disorderliness. The feeling of disorderliness is the obsession.

8. **Compulsion.** This is a compulsion which is performed to get rid of the obsession of not being clean enough.

9. **Obsession.** This is an obsession which causes fear. Avoiding children to not act upon it would be one of the compulsions.

10. **Compulsion.** This is a compulsion which is to make sure that the loved ones are safe. The thought of loved ones not being safe is the obsession.

11. **Obsession.** This is an obsession of not being clean enough. The compulsion is excessive cleaning routines in the form of long showers, repeat hand washing, etc.

12. **Obsession.** These thoughts are obsessions leading to excessive vigilance and avoidance of anything that can be a weapon. Avoidance is the compulsion.

13. **Compulsion.** This is a compulsion that may be engaged in to beat the anxiety of needing something and not having it, which is the obsession.

14. **Compulsion.** This compulsion may be to manage a specific obsession like needing to count up to a particular number to feel safe. Or it may have no reason at all.

15. **Compulsion.** This compulsion may be to handle the anxiety of making sure that a bad thought is dealt with. The bad thought is the obsession.

16. **Obsession.** This is an obsession that causes discomfort to a heterosexual. The compulsion in this case would be to constantly check if there's arousal towards the same sex.

17. **Compulsion.** This is a compulsion that is performed to deal with the anxiety of not wanting to make mistakes. The fear of making mistakes is the obsession.

18. **Obsession.** This is an obsession around feeling dirty or contaminated. The compulsion in this case would be to avoid contaminants or wash or clean excessively.

19. **Obsession.** This obsession may cause anxiety to someone who has high morals. The compulsion would be to not be alone to avoid the temptation.

20. **Obsession.** This is an obsession that involves magical thinking - connecting two unrelated things. The compulsion is to avoid doing the 'unlucky' thing.

21. **Obsession.** This is an obsession that focuses on the right and wrong according to religion or morals. The compulsion would be to not sin or do a repentance ritual.

22. **Compulsion.** This is a compulsion used to ward off bad thoughts. The bad thought that needs to be dealt with is the obsession.

23. **Obsession.** This is an obsession focusing around needing to act decently. The compulsion would be to avoid being in the public eye or keeping hand busy elsewhere.

24. **Obsession.** This is a visual obsession with images the person does not want to see - sex with family, children or God. Pushing the thought away is the compulsion.

25. **Compulsion.** This is a compulsion to make sure that there is no danger to any life or property. The obsession is the perceived danger to life or property.

26. **Compulsion.** This is a compulsion used to deal with the anxiety of an unsafe thought. The unsafe thought is the obsession.

27. **Compulsion.** Avoidance is a compulsion. The objective to not feel contaminated. This objective is the obsession.

28. **Obsession.** This is an obsession focusing around decency. The compulsion would be to avoid being in the public eye or keeping a strict check on what is being said.

29. **Compulsion.** Ordering and arranging something symmetrically is a compulsion to reduce the anxiety from disorderliness. The feeling of asymmetry is the obsession.

30. **Obsession.** The need for evenness and perfection is an obsession which may lead to repeated actions to get something down perfectly. The action is the compulsion.

31. **Obsession.** The fear of sinning is an obsession. A person may alleviate the anxiety by repeatedly praying to God and asking for forgiveness, which is the compulsion.

32. **Obsession.** The thought of being sick is an obsession which may result in compulsions of checking temperature, getting tests done, monitoring physical symptoms, etc

33. **Compulsion.** This is a compulsion involving ruminating over how

certain events transpired to ascertain if any harm was done. Causing harm is the obsession.

34. **Obsession.** This is an obsession which may lead to focusing on the rights and wrongs of things. Constant checking to make sure everything is right would be the compulsion.

35. **Compulsion.** Repeatedly praying is a compulsion. It is done to deal with the anxiety of having sinned or fear of committing a sin, which is the obsession.

36. **Compulsion.** This is a compulsion which is performed to get rid of the obsession of not being clean enough.

37. **Obsession.** This is an obsession where not remembering things causes anxiety. The compulsion is to try and remember the minute details.

38. **Compulsion.** This is a compulsion which may be done to prevent the obsession that someone may get hurt due to excessive hand movements.

39. **Compulsion.** This is reassurance seeking, which is a compulsion. Reassurance seeking is done to deal with the obsession of not being sure of one's own judgment.

40. **Obsession.** This is an obsession of harm, related to causing motor accidents and running people over. The compulsion may be to go back and check for any accidents.

Worksheet 2 - OCD Presentations Experienced

Based on the presentations of OCD outlined, identify if there are other presentations of OCD that you may be experiencing right now and please note them down. If there are any other that are not mentioned in the document, write them down too. Under the Manifestation column, write down what the presentation makes you think and do.

Sr. No.	Presentation	Manifestation
EXAMPLE	Contamination OCD	I feel that my hands are dirty and need to wash them
1		
2		
3		
4		
5		
6		
7		
8		
9		
10		
11		
12		
13		
14		
15		
16		
17		
18		
19		
20		
21		
22		
23		
24		

Worksheet 3 - Signs that you may have ROCD Type 1

Answer the following questions in Yes or No in the space provided. If you answer more than half of them with a 'Yes', and these questions cause you distress, you may have ROCD Type 1.

Sr. No.	Questions for ROCD Type 1 as compiled by Dr Jordan Levy, NYC	Yes/No
1	Do you test your level of attraction to your partner by seeing if you are more attracted to other people such as strangers, friends, exes, or celebrities?	
2	Are you constantly dwelling over your partner's physical imperfections? For example thinking things like "is his/her nose too big or eyebrows too thick/thin?"	
3	Are you constantly picking at your partner's personality? For example, thinking things like "Is he/she boring? Are his/her jokes too corny? Does he/she feel passionate about all of the same things as me? Is he/she too shy? Is he/she smart enough?"	
4	Do you shy away from dating because no one seems good enough for you?	
5	Are you unwilling to take the next step in your relationship because you are so focused on his/her flaws or because you are so focused on what is missing in the relationship?	
6	Do you constantly feel uncertain about whether or not you are in the 'right' relationship and that maybe there's someone better out there for you?	
7	Are you engaged in endless attempts to figure out just how in love you feel with your partner? For example thinking things like "Why don't I miss him/her more even though we haven't seen each other in over a week? Do I truly feel connected when we are together?"	
8	Do you seek reassurance from your friends to observe your partner's behavior and confirm to you whether your partner seems to be in love with you or not?	
9	Do you feel like you constantly need reassurance that you have made the 'right' choice in your partner?	

Sr. No.	Questions for ROCD Type 1 as compiled by Dr Jordan Levy, NYC	Yes/No
10	Are you comparing your relationship to a previous fun and exciting (often unhealthy) relationship to figure out if you feel the same way about your current partner?	
11	Are you avoiding watching romantic movies or TV shows that bring up unwanted thoughts and anxiety related to your relationships?	
12	Do you persistently look for answers on the internet and online forums?	
13	Have you found that sexual activity is a chore and a generally unpleasant and anxiety-filled event?	

Worksheet 4 - Signs that you may have ROCD Type 2

Answer the following questions in Yes or No in the space provided. If you answer more than half of them with a 'Yes', and these questions cause you distress, you may have ROCD Type 2

Sr. No.	Questions for ROCD Type 2	Yes/No
1	Do you doubt your partner's attraction towards you by checking if she seems happier with other people?	
2	Do you worry about your physical imperfections and wonder if your partner may stop loving you because of that? For example thinking things like "Am I too fat for my partner?"	
3	Do you constantly test your partner's love for you? For example, sending a text and expecting a text back immediately, or saying "I love you" just to see if she says it back exactly the way you want to hear it.	
4	Do you try to read too much meaning into your partner's words? For example do you keep wondering why she used or did not use specific words while talking to you and whether that means that she does not love you?	
5	Do you constantly feel uncertain about whether or not you are in the 'right' relationship and that maybe there's someone better out there for you who would love you the way you wanted?	
6	Do you constantly look at other couples and wonder how much in love they seem to be and why your partner cannot behave that way with you?	
7	Do you find yourself suspecting everything that your partner says and does? Do you think it is an indication that she is lying to you?	
8	Do you seek reassurance from your friends to observe your partner's behavior and confirm to you whether your partner seems to be in love with you or not?	
9	Do you constantly question your partner and seek explanations about her behavior? Does your partner feel you have become overbearing?	

Sr. No.	Questions for ROCD Type 2	Yes/No
10	Do you want to go to the next level in your relationship too fast? Do you want your partner to commit to you too soon? Do you feel insecure in your relationship at the current stage?	
11	Do you avoid watching romantic movies or TV shows that bring up unwanted thoughts and anxiety related to your relationships?	
12	Do you persistently look for answers on the internet and online forums?	
13	Do you find yourself stalking your partner's social media profiles to catch her in a lie, even though she has not given you a reason to?	
14	14. Do you think that your partner may find something bad about your past and choose to leave you?	

Worksheet 5 - Signs that you may have ROCD Type 3

Answer the following questions in Yes or No in the space provided. If you answer more than half of them with a 'Yes', and these questions cause you distress, you may have ROCD Type 3.

Sr No	Questions for ROCD Type 3	Yes/No
1	Do you doubt your relationship and think that you could be happier with someone else even though there is nothing wrong with your partner?	
2	Do you constantly worry about the correctness of committing to your partner despite everything going well?	
3	Do you think you may be making a mistake by continuing to be in a relationship with your partner?	
4	Do you check if you think of your partner often?	
5	Do you constantly find yourself wondering if you think of someone else at romantic moments?	
6	Do you keep feeling sometimes that your partner may not love you enough and hence the relationship may not be sufficient?	
7	Do you seek reassurance from your friends about the correctness of your relationship, and you have made the 'right' choice in your partner?	
8	Do you avoid watching romantic movies or TV shows that bring up unwanted thoughts and anxiety related to your relationships?	
9	Do you persistently look for answers on the internet and online forums?	
10	Do you shy away from dating because you don't know what you want from the relationship?	
11	Do you compare your relationship to a previous fun and exciting (often unhealthy) relationship to figure out if you feel the same way about your current partner?	
12	Do you find that sexual activity is a chore and generally unpleasant?	

Worksheet 6 - Cognitive Restructuring

Write down your intrusive thoughts. Identify the cognitive distortions in them. Write the statements that are cognitively restructured more adaptively, as shown in the examples.

Sr. No.	Intrusive Thought	Cognitive Distortion	Cognitive Restructuring
A	My partner should be perfect and can have no shortcomings	Black or White Thinking	No one is perfect. I am not perfect either. It is okay and for my partner to have imperfections.
B	I feel my partner is cheating on me	Emotional Reasoning	I have no evidence except that I saw her laughing with another man. I will not listen to my feelings and rely on facts instead.
C	I should always feel like she is the one for me. I should feel the love all the time	Shoulds	It is not possible to feel the love for her all the time. If I did, it would be dysfunctional. We fight and I can get angry too.
D	She did not text me on time. Maybe she does not love me. She may leave me and I will die alone.	Catastrophizing	Maybe she was busy. Not getting a text from her on time does not mean anything. I have felt this in the past and have been proven wrong.
E	My partner is in a foul mood. I wonder what I have done.	Personalization	She can be in a foul mood for other reasons as well. It may have nothing to do with me. I don't need to take it on myself and blame myself.

WORKSHEETS

1			
2			
3			
4			
5			
6			
7			
8			
9			
10			
11			
12			
13			
14			
15			
16			
17			
18			
19			
20			
21			
22			
23			
24			
25			
26			
27			
28			
29			
30			

Worksheet 7 - Things I got good at

Think back in your life starting from when you were a child. Identify 20 things that you did not know how to do. Mark 15 things that you learnt to do even if with effort. Mark 10 things that you learnt to do well with practice.

Sr No	Activities I Could Not Do	Learnt To Do	Do Very Well
A	Playing the Guitar	No	
B	Driving a Car	Yes	No
C	Walking	Yes	Yes
1			
2			
3			
4			
5			
6			

Worksheet 8 - Developing Awareness

1	Set alarms on your mobile phones at one hour intervals from the moment you wake up to the time you retire for the day.	
2	When an alarm rings, observe your thoughts. Are your actions and thoughts in alignment? Or are you doing one thing and thinking about another?	
3	Every time you are mindful, write Y in the column of the relevant day. Every time you are unmindful, write N in the column.	
4	For the times you will not set an alarm (sleeping time), write O in the corresponding cells. If you do not write O, it will be considered as a time of unmindfulness.	
5	Refer to the example provided. Write the totals of O's, Y's, N's and blank spaces. The more the Y's the better you fare.	

Time	Eg	Day 1	Day 2	Day 3	Day 4	Day 5	Day 6	Day 7
05:00	o							
06:00	o							
07:00	y							
08:00								
09:00								
10:00								
11:00								
12:00								
13:00								
14:00								
15:00	o							
16:00	o							
17:00	y							
18:00								
19:00	y							
20:00	y							
21:00	y							
22:00								
23:00								
00:00								
01:00	o							

02:00	o							
03:00	o							
04:00	o							
Omitted	8							
Aware	5							
Unaware	11							

Worksheet 9 - Things I am grateful for

Think back on your life and identify a few things that you are grateful for. A simple way to do this is to see what you have in your life that would cause discomfort if it were to be taken away. Be grateful for having them. Or think of those things which if they were introduced to your life, they could cause discomfort. Be grateful for not having them in your life. Write 3 such things in this journal every day. Let them be different each day, not the same things that you are grateful for. You will see how many things you can be grateful for that you have been ignoring.

Date	Sr. No	I am grateful for
01-01-2022	A	My partner made coffee for me this morning
01-01-2022	B	The beautiful moon last night
01-01-2022	C	My phone through which I can keep in touch with my partner

Worksheet 10 - Triggers in ROCD

Based on the cues, identify your thoughts, and write them down in the space provided. You can have more than one obsession for one cue.

Sr. No.	Cue	Trigger	Obsession
EXAMPLE	Sensory	Perfume	The perfume of an old girlfriend reminds me of her and I feel anxious that I miss her.
EXAMPLE	Cognitive	Horror Movies	Horror movies remind me of snuggling with my ex-boyfriend when I used to be scared.
EXAMPLE	Place	Chinese Restaurant	Going to a Chinese restaurant reminds me of that hot colleague from office and I am anxious.
EXAMPLE	Time of Day	Evening	When I return from office in the evening, I hate to say good bye to that new girl
EXAMPLE	Others	Yoga	When I am doing yoga, I think of having sex with that celebrity yoga teacher
1			
2			
3			
4			

Worksheet 11 - Obsessions in ROCD

1. Write the name of your ROCD in the Grey Box [   ]
2. From the Obsession Checklist identify if any obsessions apply to you and write them down in the space provided.
3. Observe yourself and identify your ROCD obsessions. Write them down in the space provided.
4. Convert the obsessions into a statement as coming from the name you have given to your ROCD.

Sr. No.	Obsessions	Distancing from Obsession
A	What if my partner is cheating on me?	Kay is telling me that my partner may be cheating on me
1		
2		
3		
4		
5		
6		
7		

Worksheet 12 - Compulsions in ROCD

1. Write the name of your ROCD in the Grey Box [   ]

2. From the Compulsion Checklist identify if any compulsions apply to you and write them down in the space provided.

3. Observe yourself and identify your ROCD compulsions. Write them down in the space provided.

4. Convert the compulsions into a statement as coming from the name you have given to your ROCD.

Sr. No.	Compulsions	Distancing from Compulsion
A	I need to confront my partner.	Kay is asking me to confront my partner
1		
2		
3		
4		
5		
6		
7		

Worksheet 13 - The Compulsion Matrix

Fill in your compulsions below and make your Compulsion Matrix (Table A)		
Pre-classification of Compulsions		
Compulsions	Unwilling / Unable	Unpleasant / Risky

Fill in your compulsions below and make your Compulsion Matrix (Table B)		
The Compulsion Matrix		
	UW	UA
U		
R		

Worksheet 14 - Contradictions in ROCD

Identify any contradictions in your ROCD as shown in the example.

Sr No		Direction	Obsession	Compulsion	Exposure
Example	A	Type 1	I don't find my partner attractive	Avoidance	**Saying "I Love You"**
	B	Type 2	My partner will leave me	**Saying "I Love You"**	Resisting seeking reassurance
1	A	Type 1			
	B	Type 2			
2	A	Type 1			
	B	Type 2			
3	A	Type 1			
	B	Type 2			
4	A	Type 1			
	B	Type 2			

Worksheet 15 - Anxiety Hierarchy

Notes before filling this format

A. Identify the presentation of OCD. The three types of ROCD are 'My partner is not good enough for me,' 'I am not good enough for my partner,' and 'Our relationship is not good enough'. For each type, a separate list will be made. Additionally, if you have identified traces of other presentations such as Contamination or Meta OCD, note them down here.

B. Identify your triggers. These triggers may be an incident, a place, an activity, a person, a memory or anything else that makes you obsess about the relationship. For example, looking at a happy couple may trigger your obsession of not being happy with your partner. You may not be able to identify a trigger for every obsession, and that is fine.

C. Identify your obsessions. Answer the following questions:

1. What are some of the distressing thoughts I get that I feel I need an answer to? For example, 'My partner has a poor sense of humor'.
2. What are the questions that I have an urgent need to find the solution to? For example, 'What if I am not in the right relationship?'
3. What images do I get most often that I don't want? For example, you may see images of your partner's nose or eyes if you obsess about them not being right.

4. What are the urges that I get that I don't want? For example, you may get the urge to break up with/ divorce your partner, or criticize her about her flaws.

D. Identify your compulsions. Answer the following questions:

1. What do I not do anymore because of ROCD that I used to do before?

2. What do I do more than I should because of ROCD that I did not used to do before?

E. Determine your SUDS score. Use the SUDS sheet given in Resource 5 to grade your fears.

Worksheet on next page

My ROCD's name (Kay / Satan or anything else) [   ]

Anxiety Hierarchy - Part A: Pre Exposure

Sr No	Presentation of OCD	Triggers	Distancing from Obsessions	SUDS	Compulsions
A	ROCD Type 1 - My partner is not good enough for me	Watching a romantic movie	KAY IS TELLING ME THAT my partner's nose is too long	8	KAY IS ASKING ME TO compare my partner's nose with other people's noses
B	ROCD Type 2 - My partner does not love me	Not getting a text immediately after I send one	KAY IS TELLING ME THAT my partner is with someone else and is cheating on me	8	KAY IS ASKING ME TO lash out at my partner, demanding to know
1					
2					
3					
4					
5					

Anxiety Hierarchy - Part B: ACTION

Date of Exposure	Beginning	10 Minutes	20 Minutes	30 Minutes	40 Minutes	50 Minutes	60 Minutes	Comments
			Anxiety Experienced					
1st January 2022	8	9	8	6	5	4		Very difficult but I could do it
4th January 2022	8	9	8	7	6	5	4	I didn't think I could do it but I did

Worksheet 16 - Rationalization of Compulsions

Rationalize each compulsion using Additional Resource 7 as a model and formulate your response prevention scripts.

A	Compulsion	
1	Rationalization (Non Triggered State)	
2	Mindful Acceptance of ROCD (Triggered State)	
3	Distancing from the Obsession (Triggered State)	
4	Distancing from the Compulsion (Triggered State)	
5	Response Prevention (Triggered State)	

B	Compulsion	
1	Rationalization (Non Triggered State)	
2	Mindful Acceptance of ROCD (Triggered State)	
3	Distancing from the Obsession (Triggered State)	
4	Distancing from the Compulsion (Triggered State)	
5	Response Prevention (Triggered State)	

Worksheet 17 - The Escape Hatch

For each of the following statements, write 'Yes' if it is a good statement for a script and 'No' if it has an escape hatch.

Sr No	Statement	Response
1	People are laughing at my partner but he does not care.	
2	I keep seeing images of having sex with the girl from my office and it is okay because I am not really attracted to her	
3	I am getting to know that my partner likes another girl and he is considering leaving me.	
4	I am speaking to my partner about her odd shaped nose and she is considering cosmetic surgery.	
5	My partner's sense of humor sucks and he is making a fool of himself.	
6	People are looking at me with pity and patronizingly when they see me with my partner.	
7	My partner is partying with other guys but they are just her friends.	
8	I feel happier with a colleague from office and I am sexually attracted to him.	
9	My partner has mentioned that he does not like how I am overweight and he's just going to have to deal with it.	
10	I just told my partner I love her and she has not responded the way I want her to.	
11	My partner does not seem to want to get married as much as I do and I am freaking out.	
12	My partner wants to get married to me soon and I am freaking out.	

Sr No	Statement	Response
13	My friend's relationship is like a fairytale for her she said, and mine isn't but it is okay.	
14	My partner has told me that he is interested in me for my money and he has never loved me.	
15	I asked my partner where she was and she is assuring me she is with her girlfriends	
16	I am checking my partner's phone and I find sexting between him and his ex girlfriend.	
17	I do a Google search and cannot conclusively find out if it is possible to have a perfect relationship.	
18	I look through my girlfriend's Instagram feed and find her sitting on her ex's lap.	
19	I am cuddling with my partner but I don't feel attracted or aroused and it is fine.	
20	My mother tells me that she still feels butterflies in her stomach when my father holds her and I don't feel the same with my partner.	

Answers to Worksheet 17 - The Escape Hatch

1. **No. Not good.** Your partner may not care but you may. And hence this is ambiguous and not good enough to use in the script, even if the escape hatch is not apparent.
2. **No. Not good.** This is a reassuring statement and hence the escape hatch exists.
3. **Yes. Good statement.** This statement is likely to cause anxiety, and it does not do anything to make the situation better.
4. **No. Not good.** There is an escape hatch in this because the situation seems to be having a way out.
5. **Yes. Good statement.** This is an anxiety inducing statement if you want your partner to make a good impression.
6. **Yes. Good statement.** This is an anxiety inducing statement if you

want people to be happy for you and your partner.

7. **No. Not good.** There is an escape hatch in this because there is a self-reassurance built in.

8. **Yes. Good statement.** This is an anxiety inducing statement that may make you feel you are disloyal to your partner.

9. **No. Not good.** There is an escape hatch in this statement because you don't care what he says about your weight.

10. **Yes. Good statement.** This is an anxiety inducing statement that may make you feel you are not loved enough by your partner.

11. **Yes. Good statement.** This is an anxiety inducing statement that may make you feel you are not loved enough by your partner.

12. **Yes. Good statement.** This is an anxiety inducing statement that may make you feel you are not ready for a commitment.

13. **No. Not good.** This statement will not cause anxiety because you accept that not having a fairytale relationship is fine.

14. **Yes. Good statement.** This is an anxiety inducing statement that may make you feel you are not loved by your partner.

15. **No. Not good.** There is an escape hatch in this statement because you are assured of your girlfriend's loyalty.

16. **Yes. Good statement.** This is an anxiety inducing statement that may make you feel you may be cheated on by your partner.

17. **Yes. Good statement.** This is an anxiety inducing statement that may make you feel you are missing out on something.

18. **Yes. Good statement.** This is an anxiety inducing statement that may make you feel you may be cheated on by your partner.

19. **No. Not good.** This statement will not cause anxiety because you accept that you will not feel the attraction all the time.

20. **Yes. Good statement.** This is an anxiety inducing statement that may make you feel that there isn't enough chemistry in the relationship.

Worksheet 18 - Interoceptive Exposure

Do the following interoceptive exposures to get habituated to the physical manifestations of your anxiety. Input your SUDS scores on successive days of exposure.

Exposure	Duration	Somatic Sensation Triggered	Thoughts Flashing	Days 1	2	3
Shake head side to side vigorously with your eyes open	30 sec	Dizziness, headache				
Pinch your nose and breathe through a straw as deeply as possible.	30 sec	Chest tightness, breathlessness, hot flashes				
Swallow quickly	10 times	Tight throat, breathlessness, dry mouth				
Hyperventilate. Stand up, breathe through your mouth and exhale hard	60 sec	Derealization, dizziness, tingling appendages				
Run in place	60 sec	Heart racing, feeling hot				
Place head between legs	30 sec	Disorientation, nausea				
Hold your breath	60 sec	Lightheadedness				
Spin (in a revolving chair, on skates, or on your feet)	30 sec	Dizziness				

Caution: If you suffer from epilepsy or seizures, cardiac conditions, asthma or lung problems, neck or back problems, or if you are pregnant, interoceptive exposures may not be right for you. Check with your doctor if these exercises will be right for you.

Worksheet 19 - Reassurance, *deassurance* and coping

Look at the statements below and categorize them as reassurance, *deassurance* or coping. Write R if the statement is a reassurance, D if the statement is a *deassurance* and C if the statement is a coping statement. A Reassurance is what you want from the world under ideal circumstances. A Deassurance is the exact opposite of a reassurance. A Coping Statement is your faith in yourself to handle pitfalls.

Sr No.	Statements	Answer
1	I am sure I have to fight this battle alone	
2	I am not making a mistake by being with my partner	
3	People are looking down at my partner	
4	My partner loves me more than anyone else	
5	I don't bother about my friends' opinions about my partner	
6	My relationship is not the best and that is fine	
7	I will handle it if I break up with my partner	
8	My partner looks good	
9	I will handle it if I am with the wrong partner	
10	I am unfaithful because I like someone else's smile	
11	My partner is poorly behaved during social engagements	
12	My partner will not leave me	
13	I am not compromising in the relationship	
14	I am not dumb	
15	I don't care if my partner does not fit-in	
16	My partner's average intelligence is irrelevant	
17	It is fine if I don't always feel good about my partner	
18	My family will approve of my choice	
19	My thoughts will not come true	
20	I don't care if my partner has a poor sense of humor	

Sr No.	Statements	Answer
21	I am unfaithful because I am attracted to someone else	
22	I am definitely unfaithful if I get sexual thoughts about my colleague	
23	My partner is not the best	
24	My relationship is not the right one for me	

Answers to Worksheet 19 - Reassurance, *deassurance* and coping

No	Statements	Answer
1	I am sure I have to fight this battle alone	D
2	I am not making a mistake by being with my partner	R
3	People are looking down at my partner	D
4	My partner loves me more than anyone else	R
5	I don't bother about my friends' opinions about my partner	C
6	My relationship is not the best and that is fine	C
7	I will handle it if I break up with my partner	C
8	My partner looks good	R
9	I will handle it if I am with the wrong partner	C
10	I am unfaithful because I like someone else's smile	D
11	My partner is poorly behaved during social engagements	D
12	My partner will not leave me	R
13	I am not compromising in the relationship	R
14	I am not dumb	R
15	I don't care if my partner does not fit-in	C
16	My partner's average intelligence is irrelevant	C
17	It is fine if I don't always feel good about my partner	C
18	My family will approve of my choice	R
19	My thoughts will not come true	R
20	I don't care if my partner has a poor sense of humor	C
21	I am unfaithful because I am attracted to someone else	D
22	I am definitely unfaithful if I get sexual thoughts about my colleague	D

No	Statements	Answer
23	My partner is not the best	D
24	My relationship is not the right one for me	D

Worksheet 20 - Reducing Reassurance Seeking

	1	Use this worksheet to reduce the number of instances of reassurance seeking
	2	Each day, write Y in the cell of the relevant day every time you seek reassurance.
	3	Add up the entries every day and write the number in the Total row. Each day, try to keep this number low and every next day, try to lower this number further.
	4	The lower this number is, the better you are at handling situations without seeking reassurance.
	5	Refer to the example provided for a better understanding.

Frequency	Eg	Day 1	Day 2	Day 3	Day 4	Day 5	Day 6	Day 7
1	Y							
2	Y							
3	Y							
4	Y							
5	Y							
6	Y							
7	Y							
8	Y							
9								
10								
11								
12								
13								
14								
15								
16								
Total	8							

References

Abramowitz, J. S., Fabricant, L. E., Taylor, S., Deacon, B. J., McKay, D., & Storch, E. A. (2014). The relevance of analogue studies for understanding obsessions and compulsions. *Clinical Psychology Review, 34*, 206-217. https://doi.org/10.1016/j.cpr.2014.01.004

Abramowitz, J.S., & Jacoby, R. J. (2015). Obsessive-compulsive and related disorders: A critical review of the new diagnostic class. *Annual Review of Clinical Psychology, 11*(1), 165–186.

Abramowitz, J. S., McKay, D., and Taylor, S. (2008). *Obsesif-kompulsifbozuklukvebağlantılısorunlarklinikelkitabı*. Çev. Y. B. Doğan ve O. Karamustafaoğlu. İstanbul: Okuyan Us Yayın

American Psychiatric Association (2013). *Diagnostic and statistical manual of mental disorders (5th ed.)*. USA.

Behan, C. (2020). The benefits of meditation and mindfulness practices during times of crisis such as COVID-19. *Irish Journal of Psychological Medicine, 37*(4), 256-258. https://doi.org/10.1017/ipm.2020.38

Benito, K. G., Machan, J., Freeman, J. B., Garcia, A. M., Walther, M., Frank, H., Wellen, B., Stewart, E., Edmunds, J., Kemp, J., Sapyta, J., & Franklin, M. (2018). Measuring fear change within exposures: Functionally-defined habituation predicts outcome in three randomized controlled trials for pediatric OCD. *Journal of Consulting and Clinical Psychology, 86*(7), 615–630. https://doi.org/10.1037/ccp0000315

Benjamin, C. L., O'Neil, K. A., Crawley, S. A., Beidas, R. S., Coles, M., & Kendall, P. C. (2010). Patterns and predictors of subjective units of distress in anxious youth. *Behavioural and cognitive psychotherapy, 38*(04), 497-504.

Bond, F. W., Hayes, S. C., Baer, R. A., Carpenter, K. M., Guenole, N., Orcutt, H. K., Waltz, T., & Zettle, R. D. (2011). Preliminary psychometric properties of the Acceptance and Action Questionnaire-II: A revised measure of psychological inflexibility and experiential avoidance. *Behavior Therapy, 42*(4), 676-688. https://doi.org/10.1016/j.beth.2011.03.007

Brandt, L., Bschor, T., Henssler, J., Müller, M., Hasan, A., Heinz, A., & Gutwinski, S. (2020). Antipsychotic withdrawal symptoms: A systematic review and meta-analysis. *Frontiers in Psychiatry, 11*, https://www.doi.org/10.3389/fpsyt.2020.569912

Brown, A. D. (2017). Toxic relationship: Being aware of the effects of a dysfunctional relationship. *Psychology Today.* https://www.psychologytoday.com/us/blog/towards-recovery/201709/toxic-relationships

Brown, K.W. & Ryan, R.M. (2003). The benefits of being present: Mindfulness and its role in psychological well-being. *Journal of Personality and Social Psychology, 84*, 822-848.

Burchi, E., Hollander, E., & Pallanti, S. (2018). From treatment response to recovery: A realistic goal in OCD. *International Journal of Neuropsychopharmacology, 21*(11), 1007–13. https://doi.org/10.1093/ijnp/pyy079.

Butchler, J. N., Mineka, S., ve Hooley,& J. M. (2013). *Anormal Psikoloji.* Çev. O. Gündüz. İstanbul: Kaknüs Yayınları.

Clark, D. M. (1986). A cognitive approach to panic. *Behaviour Research and Therapy, 24*, 461–470.

Coles, M. E., & Ravid, A. (2016). Clinical presentation of not-just right experiences (NJREs) in individuals with OCD: Characteristics and response to treatment. *Behaviour Research and Therapy, 87*, 182–187. https://doi.org/10.1016/j.brat.2016.09.013

Coughtrey, A., Shafran, R., Knibbs, D., & Rachman, S. (2012). Mental contamination in obsessive–compulsive disorder. *Journal of Obsessive-Compulsive and Related Disorders, 1*(4), 244–250. https://doi.org/10.1016/j.jocrd.2012.07.006

Dahl, R. E., & Harvey, A. G. (2007). Sleep in children and adolescents with behavioral and emotional disorders. *Sleep Medicine Clinics, 2*(3), 501-511.

Dodson, C. S., Koutstaal, W., & Schacter, D. L. (2000). Escape from illusion: Reducing false memories. *Trends in Cognitive Sciences, 4*(10), 391-397. https://doi.org/10.1016/S1364-6613(00)01534-5

Doron, G., Derby, D. S., Szepsenwol, O., & Talmor, D. (2012a). Flaws and all: Exploring partner-focused obsessive-compulsive symptoms. *Journal of Obsessive-Compulsive and Related Disorders, 1*(4), 234-243. https://doi.org/10.1016/j.jocrd.2012.05.004.

Doron, G., Derby, D. S., Szepsenwol, O., & Talmor, D. (2012b). Tainted love: Exploring relationship-centered obsessive compulsive symptoms in two non-clinical cohorts. *Journal of Obsessive-Compulsive and Related Disorders, 1*(1), 16-24. https://doi.org/10.1016/j.jocrd.2011.11.002.

Doron, G., Derby, D., & Szepsenwol, O. (2017). 'I can't stop thinking about my child's flaws': An investigation of parental preoccupation with their children's perceived flaws. *Journal of obsessive-compulsive and related disorders, 14*, 106-111.

Einstein, D. A., & Menzies, R. G. (2004). Role of magical thinking in obsessive-compulsive symptoms in an undergraduate sample. *Depression and Anxiety, 19*(3), 174-179. https://doi.org/10.1002/da.20005.

Eisen, J. L., Phillips, K. A., Beer, D. A., Atala, K. D., & Rasmussen, S. A. (1998). The Brown Assessment of Beliefs Scale: Reliability and validity. Am J Psychiatry, 155, 102-108.

Farrrell, N. (2021, April 14). What is real event OCD? *Treat My OCD.* https://www.treatmyocd.com/blog/real-events-ocd

Fava, G. A., Gatti, A., Belaise, C., Guidi, J., & Offidani, E. (2015). Withdrawal symptoms after selective serotonin reuptake inhibitor discontinuation: A systematic review. *Psychotherapy and Psychosomatics, 84,* 72–81. https://doi.org/10.1159/000370338

Filer, A.D.J., & Brockington, I.F. (1996). Maternal obsessions of child sexual abuse. *Psychopathology, 29*(2), 135–138.

REFERENCES

Foa, E. B., Liebowitz, M. R., Kozak, M. J., Davies, S., Campeas, R., Franklin, M. E., et al. (2005). Randomized, placebo-controlled trial of exposure and ritual prevention, clomipramine, and their combination in the treatment of Obsessive-Compulsive disorder. *The American Journal of Psychiatry, 162*, 151–161.

Geller, D. A., McGuire, J. F., Orr, S. P., Small, B. J., Murphy, T. K., Trainor, K., Porth, R., Wilhelm, S., & Storch, E. A. (2019). Fear extinction learning as a predictor of response to cognitive behavioral therapy for pediatric obsessive compulsive disorder. *Journal of Anxiety Disorders, 64*, 1–8. https://doi.org/10.1016/j.janxdis.2019.02.005

Germer, C. K., Siegel, R. D., & Fulton, P. R. (Eds.). (2005). *Mindfulness and Psychotherapy.* USA: Guilford.

Gillihan, S. J., Williams, M. T., Malcoun, E., Yadin, E., & Foa, E. B. (2012). Common pitfalls in exposure and response prevention (EX/RP) for OCD. *Journal of Obsessive-Compulsive and Related Disorders, 1*(4), 251-257. https://doi.org/10.1016/j.jocrd.2012.05.002.

Goetz, J. E., Keltner, D., Simon-Thomas, E. (2010). Compassion: An evolutionary analysis and empirical review. *Psychological Bulletin, 136*, 351–374.

González-Ortega, I., Echeburúa, E., & De Corral, P. (2008). Significant variables in violent dating relationships in young couples: A review. *Psicología Conductual, 16*, 207–222.

Goodman, W. K., Grice, D. E., Lapidus, K. A. B., & Coffey, B. J. (2014). Obsessive-Compulsive Disorder. *Psychiatric Clinics of North America, 37*(3), 257-267. https://doi.org/10.1016/j.psc.2014.06.004.

Goodman, W. K., Price, L H., Rasmussen, S. A., Mazure, C, Delgado, P., Heninger, G. R., & Charney, D. S. (1989a). The Yale-Brown Obsessive Compulsive Scale. II. Validity. *Archives of General Psychiatry, 46*, 1012-1016. https://www.doi.org/10.1001/archpsyc.1989.01810110054008

Goodman, W. K., Price, L. H., Rasmussen, S. A., Mazure, C., Fleischmann, R. L., Hill, C. L., Heninger, G. R., & Charney, D. S. (1989b). The Yale-Brown Obsessive Compulsive Scale I. *Archives of General Psychiatry, 46*, 1006-1011. https://osf.io/tn2vg/download

Grayson, J., & Price, M. (2021). Ocular Tourettic OCD. *IOCDF OCD Newsletter, 35*(1), 19. https://iocdf.org/wp-content/uploads/2017/07/IOCDF-OCD-Newsletter-Spring-2021.pdf

Griffin, C. E., Kaye, A. M., Bueno, F. R., & Kaye, A. D. (2013) Benzodiazepine pharmacology and central nervous system–mediated effects. *Ochsner Journal, 13*(2), 214–223.

Greenberg, D., & Huppert, J. D. (2010). Scrupulosity: A unique subtype of obsessive-compulsive disorder. *Current Psychiatry Reports, 12*, 282–289.

Haverkampf, C. J. (2017). *Pure 'O' OCD and psychotherapy.*

Hayes, S. C., Strosahl, K. D., Bunting, K., Twohig, M., & Wilson, K. G. (2004). What is acceptance and commitment therapy?. In *A practical guide to acceptance and commitment therapy* (pp. 3-29). Springer, Boston, MA.

Hoffmann, K., Emons, B., Brunnhuber, S., Karaca, S., & Juckel, G. (2019). The role of dietary supplements in depression and anxiety–a narrative review. *Pharmacopsychiatry, 52*(06), 261-279.

Jans-Beken, L., Jacobs, N., Janssens, M., Peeters, S., Reijnders, J., Lechner, L., & Lataster, J. (2020). Gratitude and health: An updated review. *The Journal of Positive Psychology, 15*(6), 743-782. https://doi.org/10.1080/17439760.2019.1651888

Julien, D., O'Connor, K. P., & Aardema, F. (2009). Intrusions related to obsessive–compulsive disorder: A question of content or context? *Journal of Clinical Psychology, 65*(7), 709–722. https://doi.org/10.1002/jclp.20578

Kabat-Zinn, J. (1994). *Wherever You Go, There You Are: Mindfulness Meditation in Everyday Life*. USA: Hyperion

Kabat-Zinn, J. (2013). The foundations of mindfulness practice: *Attitudes and commitment. Full Catastrophe Living: Using the Wisdom of Your Mind to Face Stress, Pain and Illness*, 19-38. USA: Random House.

Karam, E. A., Antle, B. F., Stanley, S. M., & Rhoades, G. K. (2015). The marriage of couple and relationship education to the practice of marriage and family therapy: A primer for integrated training. *Journal of Couple and Relationship Therapy, 14*, 277–295. https://doi.org/10.1080/15332691.2014.100265.

Kaufman, I. (2021, October 22). *How to control death*. Psychology Today. https://www.psychologytoday.com/us/blog/the-beginning-the-end/202110/how-control-death

Keuler, D. J. (2011). When automatic bodily processes become conscious: How to disengage from 'Sensorimotor Obsessions'. *IOCDF OCD Newsletter*.

Khodarahimi, S. (2009). Satiation therapy and exposure and response prevention in the treatment of obsessive compulsive disorder. *Journal of Contemporary Psychotherapy, 39*(3), 203–7. https://www.doi.org/10.1007/s10879-009-9110-z.

Kluchka, A. A. (2021). *Psychology in Marketing: The Baader-Meinhof Phenomenon*. ББК 65.42 С76, 12.

Kuru, E., Safak, Y., Özdemir, İ., Tulacı, R. G., Özdel, K., Özkula, N. G., & Örsel, S. (2018). Cognitive distortions in patients with social anxiety disorder: Comparison of a clinical group and healthy controls. *The European Journal of Psychiatry, 32*(2), 97-104. https://doi.org/10.1016/j.ejpsy.2017.08.004

Lee, H.J., & Kwon, S.-M. (2003). Two different types of obsessions: Autogenous obsessions and reactive obsessions. *Behaviour Research and Therapy, 41*, 11–29.

Marais, S. D. (2020, May 12). *1, 2, 3: Counting and OCD*. Impulse Therapy. https://impulsetherapy.com/1-2-3-counting-and-ocd/

Matheson, L. (2014). *Your Faithful Brain: Designed for So Much More!* WestBow Press.

McKay, D., Sookman, D., Neziroglu, F., Wilhelm, S., Stein, D. J., Kyrios, M., Matthews, K., & Veale, D. (2015). Efficacy of cognitive behavioral therapy for obsessive-compulsive disorder. *Psychiatry Research, 225*(3), 236–246. https://doi.org/10.1016/j.psychres.2014.11.058

REFERENCES

Milliner-Oar, E., Cadman, J., & Farrell, L. (2016) *Treatment of aggressive obsessions in childhood obsessive-compulsive disorder.* In: Storch E., Lewin A. (eds) Clinical Handbook of Obsessive-Compulsive and Related Disorders. Springer, Cham. https://doi.org/10.1007/978-3-319-17139-5_11

Moulding, R., Aardema, F., & O'Connor, K. P. (2014). Repugnant obsessions: A review of the phenomenology, theoretical models, and treatment of sexual and aggressive obsessional themes in OCD. *Journal of Obsessive-Compulsive and Related Disorder, 3,* 161-168.

Myers, S. G., Fisher, P. L., and Wells, A. (2009). An empirical test of the metacognitive model of obsessive-compulsive symptoms: fusion beliefs, beliefs about rituals, and stop signals'. *Journal of anxiety disorders, 23*(4), 436-442.

Myers, S. G. & Wells, A. (2005). Obsessive-compulsive symptoms: the contribution of metacognitions and responsibility. *Journal of Anxiety Disorders, 19*(7), 806-817. https://doi.org/10.1016/j.janxdis.2004.09.004

Neff, K. D. (2003). Development and validation of a scale to measure self-compassion. *Self and Identity, 2,* 223-250.

Obi, J. S. C., & Oguzie, A. E. (2019). Effects of systematic desensitization technique on generalized anxiety among adolescents in Enugu East Local Government. Enugu State, Nigeria. *iJournals: International Journal of Social Relevance & Concern, 7*(5), 1-9. https://www.shorturl.at/gvFIQ

Palmer, A.M., Schlauch, R.C., & Darkes, S. (2019). Treatment of violent and sexual obsessions using exposure and response prevention during a concurrent depressive episode. *Clinical Case Studies, 18*(3), 220–234.

Penzel, F. (2013). To be or not to be, that is the obsession: Existential and philosophical OCD. *IOCDF OCD Newsletter.*

Pinciotti, C. M., Riemann, B. C. & Abramowitz, J. S. (2021). Intolerance of uncertainty and obsessive-compulsive disorder dimensions. *Journal of Anxiety Disorders, 81,* 102417. https://doi.org/10.1016/j.janxdis.2021.102417.

Pinto, A., Van Noppen, B., & Calvocoressi, L. (2012). Development and preliminary psychometric evaluation of a self-rated version of the Family Accommodation Scale for Obsessive-Compulsive Disorder. Journal of Obsessive-Compulsive and Related Disorders. https://ysph.yale.edu/familyaccommodationocd/

Prudovski, A. (n.d.). *Don't argue with a brain glitch. (10 do's and 5 don'ts for parents of kids with OCD).* Turning Point Psychology. https://www.turningpointpsychology.ca/blog/children-with-ocd-guidelines-for-parents

Rachman, S., & Hodgson, R. (1980). *Obsessions and compulsions.* USA: Prentice-Hall

Rachman, S. (2004). Fear of contamination. *Behaviour Research and Therapy, 42*(11), 1227–1255. https://doi.org/10.1016/j.brat.2003.10.009

Rachman, S. (2007). *Treating religious, sexual, and aggressive obsessions.* In M.M. Antony, C. Purdon, & L.J. Summerfeldt (Eds.), Psychological Treatment of Obsessive-Compulsive Disorder: Fundamentals and Beyond. American Psychological Association. pp. 209–229.

Radomsky, A. S., & Rachman, S. (2004). Symmetry, ordering and arranging compulsive behavior. *Behaviour Research and Therapy, 42*(8), 893-913, https://doi.org/10.1016/j.brat.2003.07.001

Ratey, J. J. (2019, October, 24). *Can exercise help treat anxiety?* Health Harvard. https://www.health.harvard.edu/blog/can-exercise-help-treat-anxiety-2019102418096

Robbins, T. W., Vaghi, M. M., & Banca, P. (2019). Obsessive-Compulsive Disorder: Puzzles and Prospects. *Neuron, 102*(1) - 27-47. https://doi.org/10.1016/j.neuron.2019.01.046.

Robinson, J. (2021, September 14). *Foods to avoid if you have anxiety or depression.* Web MD. https://www.webmd.com/depression/ss/slideshow-avoid-foods-anxiety-depression

Seyfer, W. S. (2021). *Misunderstood: Phenomenologically Informed Research of Illness Experiences of Individuals with' Pure O' OCD.* Scholar Works. https://scholarworks.uvm.edu/cgi/viewcontent.cgi?article=1119&context=castheses

Siev, J., Baer, L. & Minichiello, W. E. (2011). Obsessive-compulsive disorder with predominantly scrupulous symptoms: clinical and religious characteristics. *Journal of Clinical Psychology, 67*, 1188–1196.

Strasser, B., Gostner, J. M., & Fuchs, D. (2016). Mood, food, and cognition: Role of tryptophan and serotonin. *Current Opinion in Clinical Nutrition & Metabolic Care, 19*(1), 55-61. https://www.doi.org/10.1097/MCO.0000000000000237

Szepsenwol, O., Shahar, B., & Doron, G. (2016). Letting it linger: Exploring the longitudinal effects of relationship-related obsessive-compulsive phenomena. *Journal of Obsessive-Compulsive and Related Disorders, 11*, 101-104. https://doi.org/10.1016/j.jocrd.2016.10.001.

Tripathi, A., Avasthi, A., Grover, S., Sharma, E., Lakdawala, B.M., Thirunavukarasu, M., Dan, A., Sinha, V., Sareen, H., Mishra, K. K., Rastogi, P., Srivastava S., Dhingra, I., Behere, P. B., Solanki, R. K., Sinha, V. K., Desai, M., & Reddy, Y. C. J. (2018). Gender differences in obsessive-compulsive disorder: Findings from a multicentric study from India. *Asian Journal of Psychiatry, 37*, 3–9. https://doi.org/10.1016/j.ajp.2018.07.022

VanDalfsen, G. (2020, September 2). *Counting OCD: Why do I always count?* Treat My OCD. https://www.treatmyocd.com/blog/counting-numbers-ocd

Vaughn, D. (2020, September 8). *Suicidal OCD: Thoughts, obsessions & treatment.* Treat My OCD. https://www.treatmyocd.com/blog/suicidal-ocd

Whiteside, S. P., Deacon, B. J., Benito, K., & Stewart, E. (2016). Factors associated with practitioners' use of exposure therapy for childhood anxiety disorders. *Journal of Anxiety Disorders, 40*, 29–36.

Williams, M. T., Mugno, B., Franklin, M., & Faber, S. (2013). Symptom dimensions in obsessive-compulsive disorder: Phenomenology and treatment outcomes with exposure and ritual prevention. *Psychopathology, 46*(6), 365–376.

Wolpe, J. (1954). Reciprocal inhibition as the main basis of psychotherapeutic effects. *Archives of Neurology and Psychiatry, 72*, 205–226

REFERENCES

World Health Organization (2017). *Violence against women*. Retrieved from
https://www.who.int/news-room/factsheets/detail/violence-against-women

Wortmann, F. (2014, March 26). *Obsessing about obsessing: When OCD goes meta*.
Psychology Today.
https://www.psychologytoday.com/us/blog/triggered/201403/obsessing-about-obsessing-when-ocd-goes-meta

Websites

Love is Respect: www.loveisrespect.org

The University of Sydney: https://www.sydney.edu.au/

SGI USA World Tribune - May 2018: https://www.sgi-usa.org

University of Michigan Health: https://www.uofmhealth.org/

Made in the USA
Coppell, TX
23 October 2024

39094175R00148